# CONTEMPORARY BRITISH ARCHITECTURAL DRAWING

# CONTEMPORARY BRITISH ARCHITECTURAL DRAWING

COVER ILLUSTRATION  by Zaha Hadid

First published in Great Britain in 1993 by
ACADEMY EDITIONS
An imprint of the Academy Group Ltd.

ACADEMY GROUP LTD
42 Leinster Gardens, London W2 3AN
ERNST & SOHN
Hohenzollerndamm 170, 1000 Berlin 31
Members of VCH Publishing Group

ISBN 1-85490-193-1

Editorial Director: Kakuzo Akahira
Book Designer: Toru Kaiho

Originally published in Japan in 1993 by
CREO CORPORATION
© 1993 Creo Corporation
8F, Nanpeidai Tokyu Building, 1-21-6 Dogenzaka, Shibuya-ku, Tokyo 150, Japan


Printed in Japan

# CONTENTS

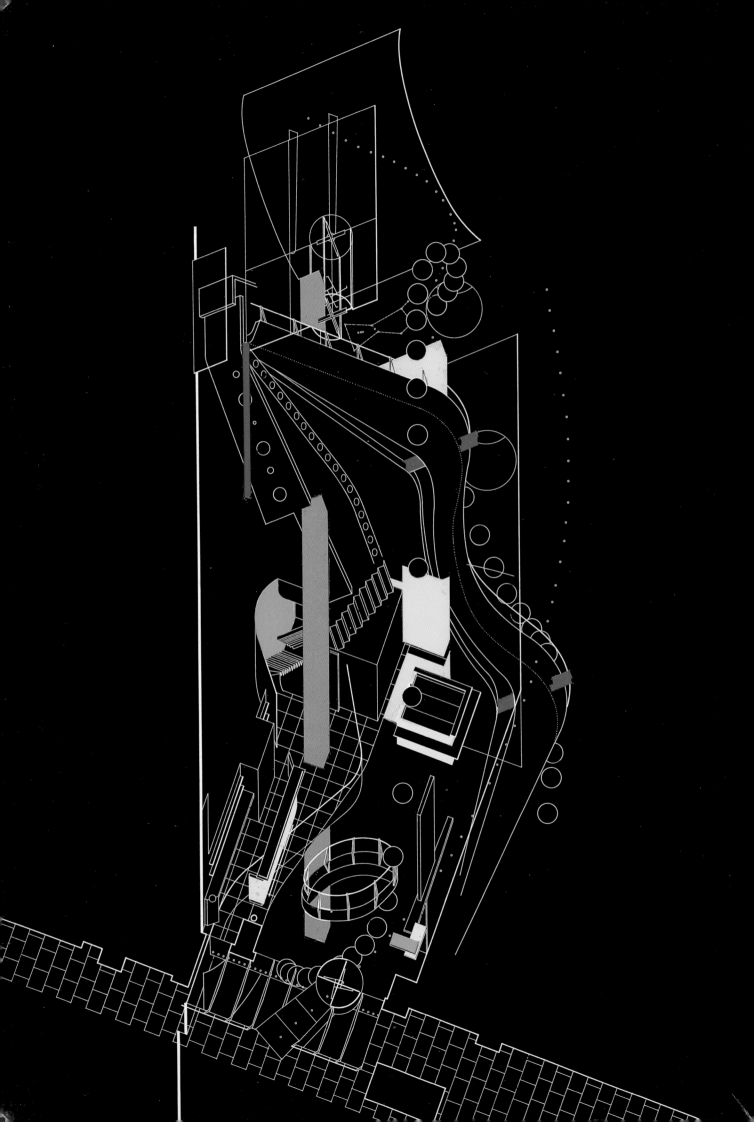

# BRITISH ARCHITECTURAL DRAWING
## PETER WILSON

In England, almost more than in any other country, architectural drawing manners extend beyond the conventional canons of architecture to overlap with other general cultural fields such as fashion illustration, science fiction, car maintenance (although the French downgrade the high-tech genre to the level of 'bicycle building'), weekend painting and/or high art.

Much admired English pragmatism, with its inbuilt mistrust for systems and rules, is largely responsible for this inability to define, let alone stay within, limits that in other countries are considered to give architecture its priority. For this reason neither modernism nor any other subsequent and less durable 'ism' has suceeded in taking root.

Such infinite licence makes it very difficult to ensure the value of genuinely consequent architectural drawing, that is drawing as the flux and vehicle of architectural conception. Even in a book such as this, one must look critically and separate this higher order of architectural drawing from mere whimsy, modishness or professional cynicism.

The extremes of pleasure and guilt that accompany the severing of the drawing itself from a still vaguely moralistic chain of causality – from need to conception (drawing) to realisation (building) – are particulary polarised in the English situation. When Archigram drew cities that walked, they were closer to the comic strip than to Lutyens' definition of a drawing as a letter to the builder. Their images outraged the architectural profession. That same profession now traces the lineage of buildings such as Lloyds of London back twenty years to the drawings of Archigram. But all that was then drawn walking and plugging-in needs no retrospective justification. These were perhaps the first truly autonomous English architectural drawings, that is, drawings which shoulder architecture's responsibility for cultural renewal.

Integral to this dangerous concept of a higher order of architectural drawing is this requirement for a work to be an agent for polemic critique. Archigram produced odes to the machine, the same mechanism which inspired heroic modernism. The inheritors of this tradition have today refined the technological genre to a level of detail fetish. The bolt and gasket have been overtaken as an appropriate 'aestheticisation' of today's technology by invisible tele-computer technology. Drawings emanating from the mechanical tradition tend to be illustrative but not generative, with the exception perhaps of future systems which continue with space-shot optimism to produce visions of a technology that solves all problems.

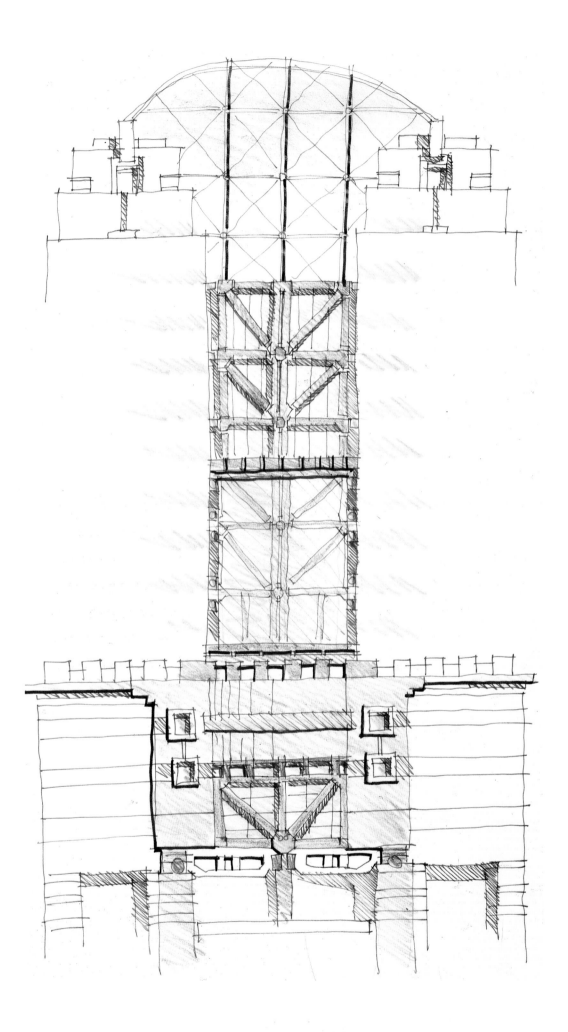

Curiously, as new technologies reformulate our perception of object and surface, such dogged pursuit of the unambiguous mega-object may again come to the architectural forefront.

The pursuit of the cult of drawing is a charge often levelled against the staff and students of the Architectural Association, but the real crime is that the AA is 'un-English'; a paradox as the majority of English architectural imagery emanates from this source. While they were there, Elia Zenghelis and Rem Koolhaas produced polemic and drawn manifestos which have provided a groundstone for our contemporary understanding of modernism. From this base, Zaha Hadid's subsequent anti-gravity flights have projected a whole new field of composition. Bernard Tschumi's connections between cinematic sequencing, architecture and post-structuralist theory also originated with his AA teachings and Daniel Libeskind's 'Chamberwork Drawings', first exhibited at the AA, have influenced a subsequent regeneration of architecture as representation of thought.

Although all this happened in England and is of great influence internationally, it is unfortunately not the base for an English tradition, drawn or built.

Subsequent AA products, many of which are seen in this book, are less focused ideologically but are nonetheless provocative, producing connections between the realm of idea and the realm of material and object. The emergence of the trans-avant garde in early eighties painting was translated into the anarchic urbanism of wild sketching. Today, this genre has been diluted by fashion and media. The hothouse of high street commercialism offers the young architect in England the possibility of building interiors but very little else. It is not surprising that many young talents survive on the edge of a momentary design world and do not evolve more mature architectural strategies. Drawings in this field are about illustration and selling but rarely about ideas.

Finally, one must see what is produced in England today, especially the new and little published AA generation, against the background of an unbelievably conservative architectural climate. Until the impossibility of this English nostalgic fantasy is played out, we must hope that in architectural drawing at least a genuine, contemporary, critical and inventive architecture will survive.

# THE ARCHITECTS

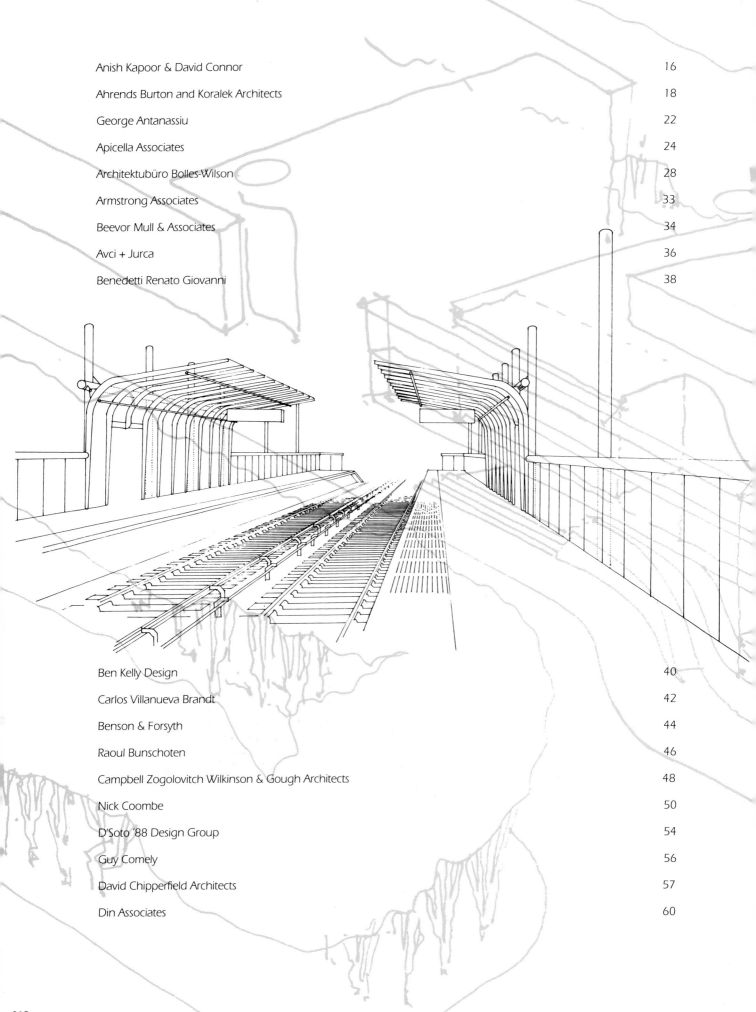

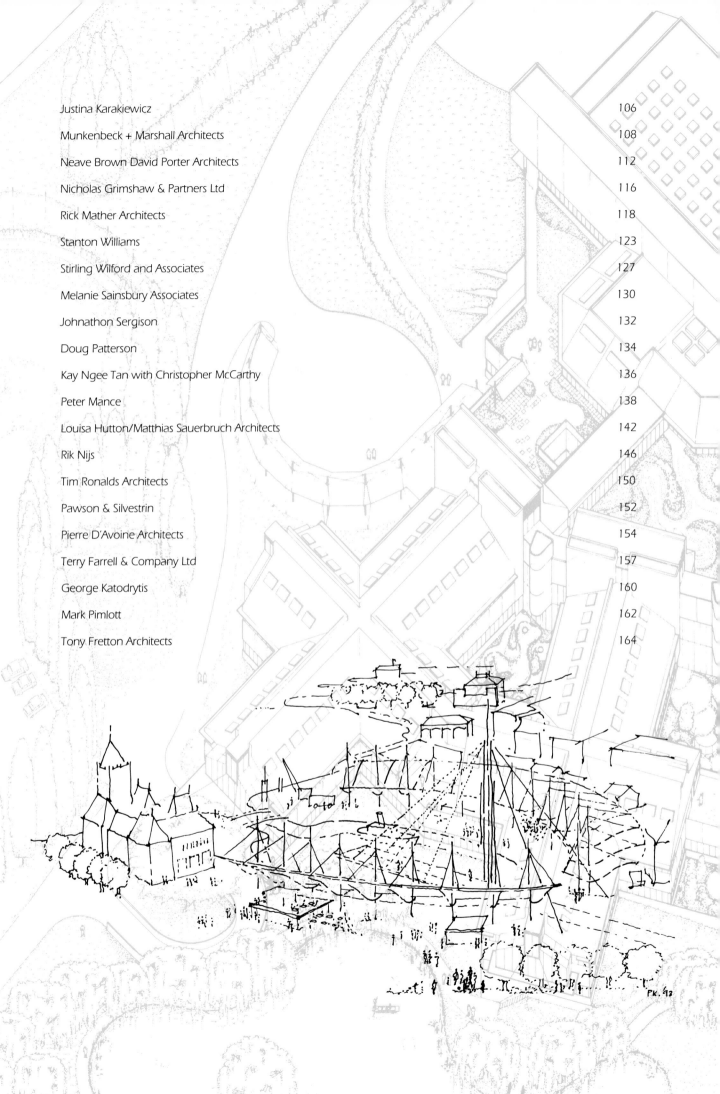

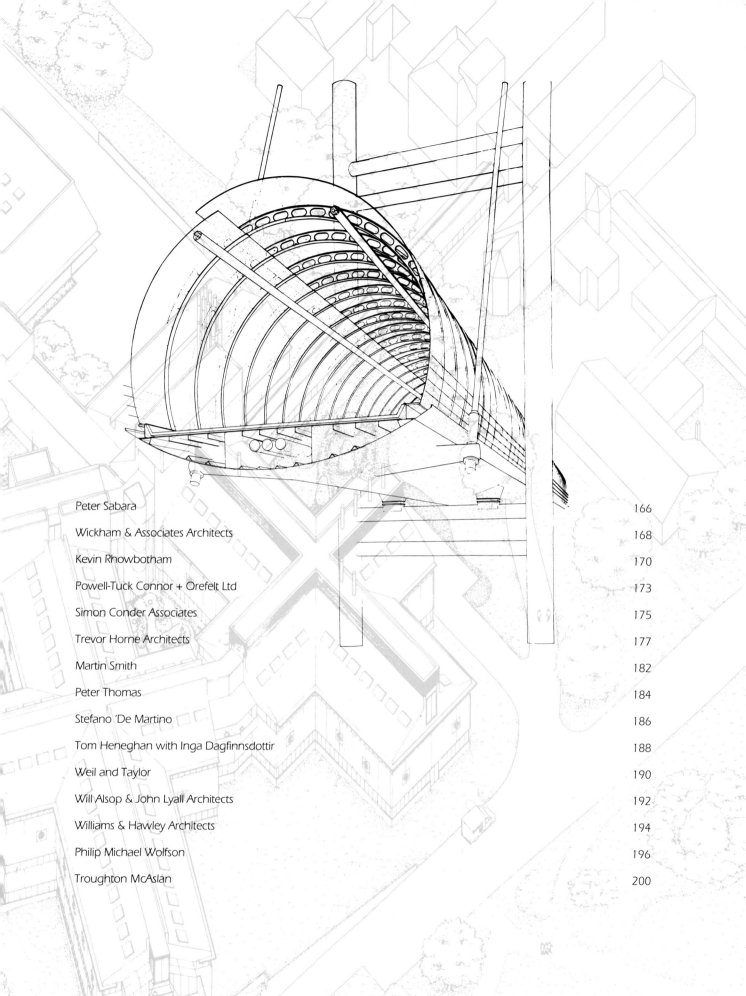

# Anish Kapoor & David Connor

Title———Building For a Void
Material—pencil, emulsion paint, oil paint
Size———3000×3000mm
Design——Anish Kapoor
Drawing—David Connor

The building is generated around a void to present its juxtaposition in an elemental relationship with the earth and sky. It is a slightly tapering elliptical structure covered in rough stucco and is entered on a spiral ramp which hugs its shape. The "void" is apparent between the rough stone slabs of the floor and the circular opening in the 8 meter domed polished plaster roof.

# Ahrends Burton and Koralek Architects

Title——British Rail North Pole Depot
Material—ink, crayon
Size——841×1189mm

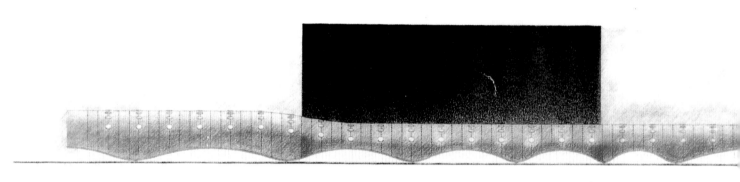

EAST ELEVATION

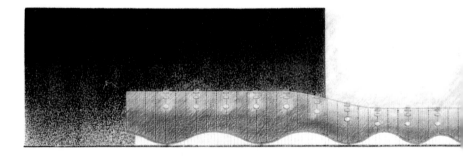

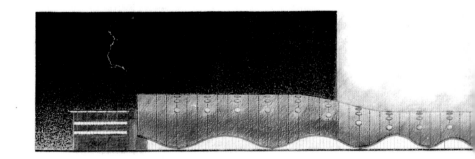

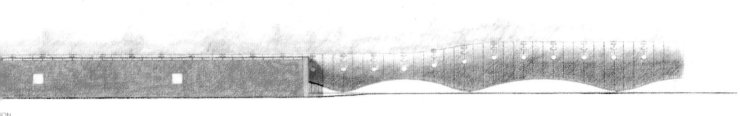

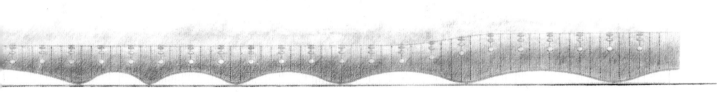

ION

HED

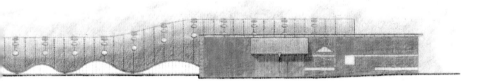

ION

WEST ELEVATION

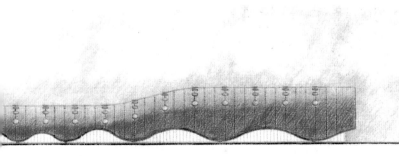

ION

ED

This project comprises a number of buildings as part of a major new depot to service the channel tunnel trains. The buildings range in size from the servicing shed which is over 400 metres long by approximately 38 metres wide, to the relatively small gatehouse.

The servicing shed, which is designed to contain a maximum of six full train sets, will house the activities related to fast turn around of the trains on a daily basis.

Major aspects of train maintenance and repair will be dealt with in the repair shed, which is approximately half the size of the servicing shed, large enough to house four half train sets at one time. Both the servicing and the repair sheds have associated amenity and stores functions and these are housed adjacent to the sheds.

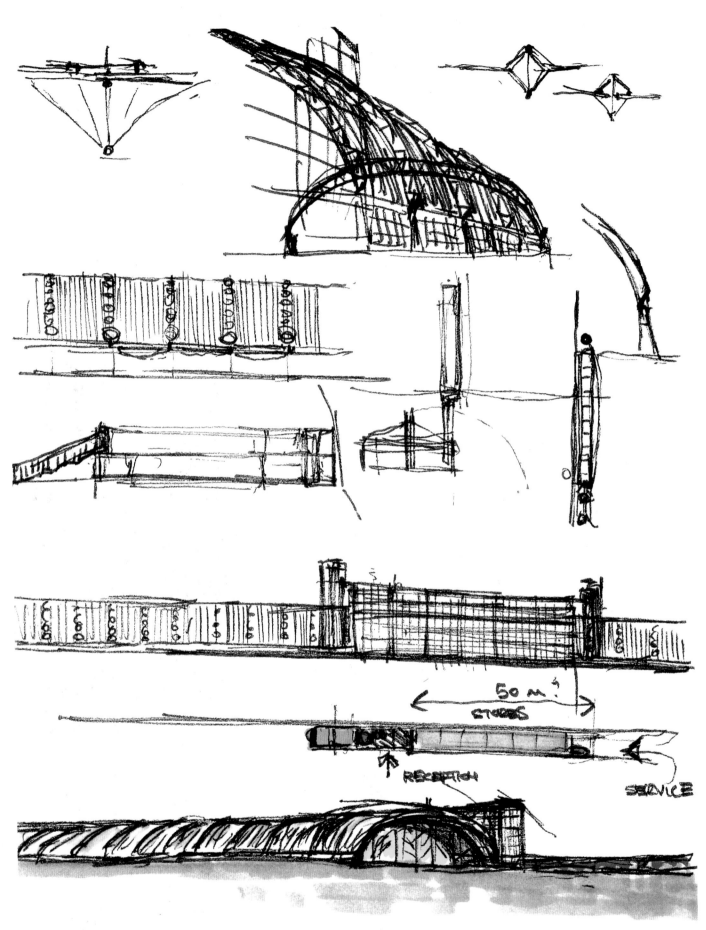

50 m.

STORES

RECEPTION

SERVICE

Title———British Rail North Pole Depot
Material—watercolour
Size———297×210mm

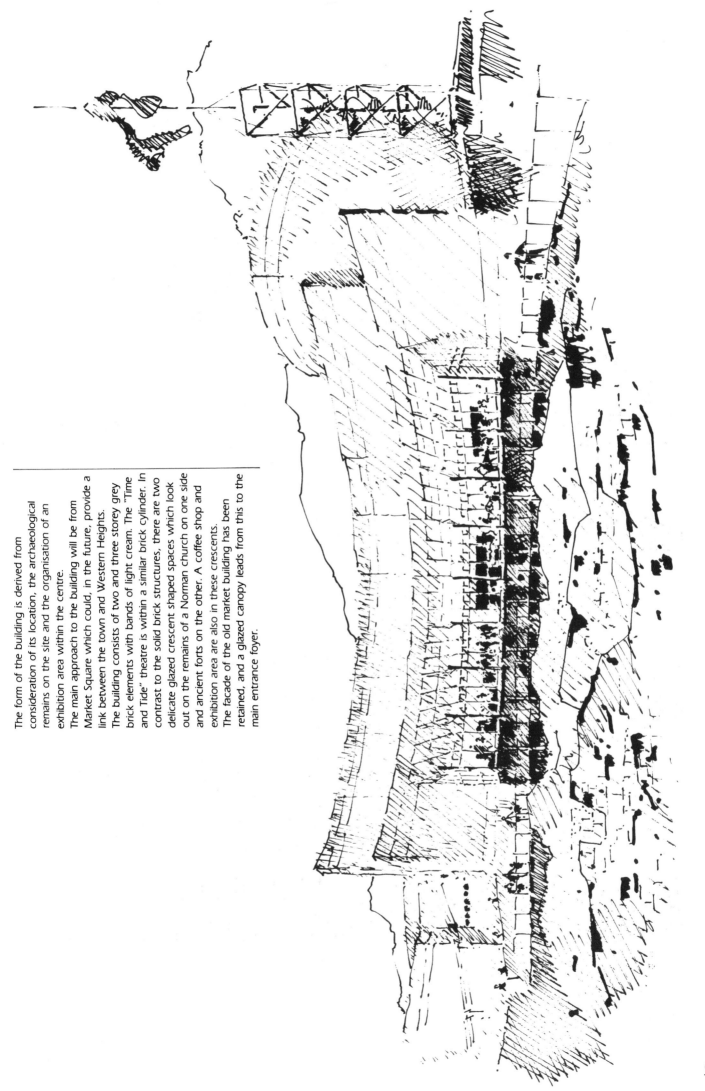

The form of the building is derived from consideration of its location, the archaeological remains on the site and the organisation of an exhibition area within the centre.

The main approach to the building will be from Market Square which could, in the future, provide a link between the town and Western Heights.

The building consists of two and three storey grey brick elements with bands of light cream. The "Time and Tide" theatre is within a similar brick cylinder. In contrast to the solid brick structures, there are two delicate glazed crescent shaped spaces which look out on the remains of a Norman church on one side and ancient forts on the other. A coffee shop and exhibition area are also in these crescents.

The facade of the old market building has been retained, and a glazed canopy leads from this to the main entrance foyer.

# George Antanassiu

Title———The Master's House, A Place for Tai-Chi
Material—ink, tracing paper
Size———634×982mm(each)

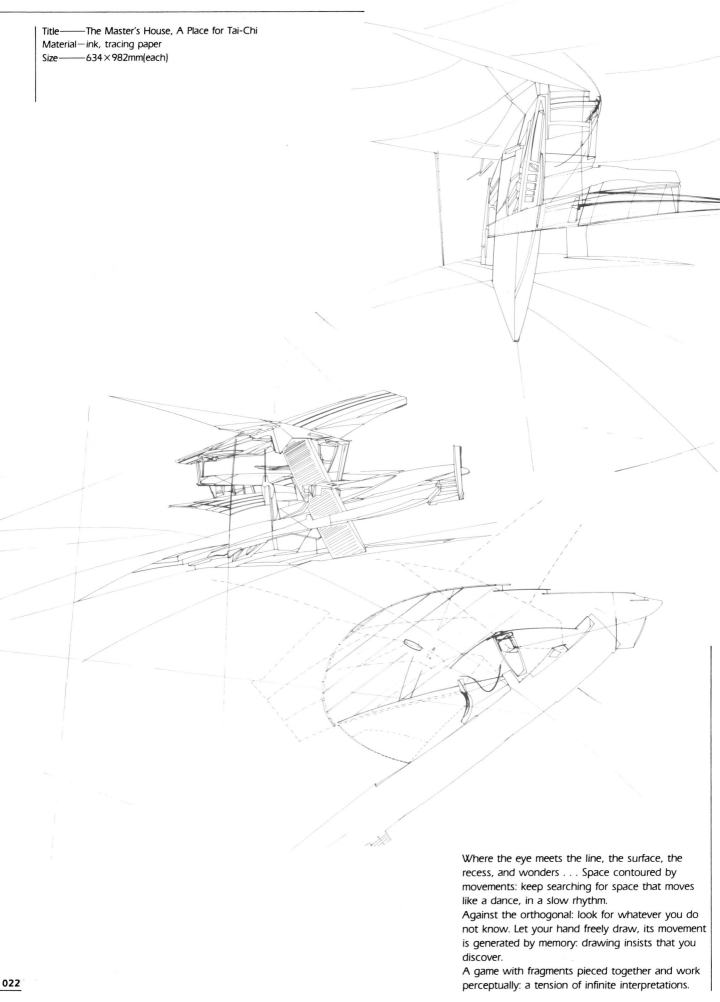

Where the eye meets the line, the surface, the recess, and wonders . . . Space contoured by movements: keep searching for space that moves like a dance, in a slow rhythm.
Against the orthogonal: look for whatever you do not know. Let your hand freely draw, its movement is generated by memory: drawing insists that you discover.
A game with fragments pieced together and work perceptually: a tension of infinite interpretations.

# Apicella Associates

Title———New Offices on the South Bank, London
Material—ink, acrylic, film
Size———400×400mm

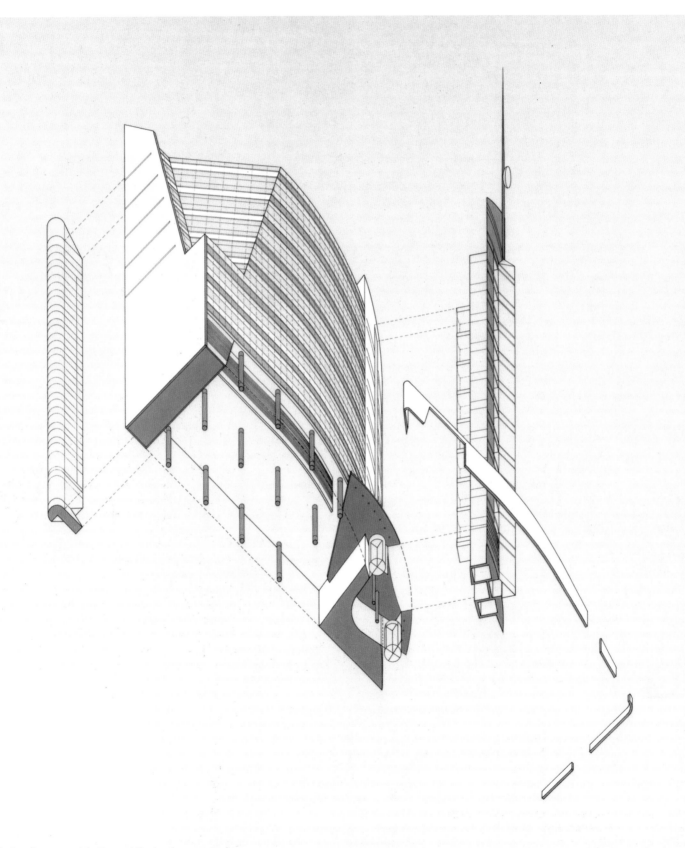

A drawing to explain the architectural concept of
carefully composed but clearly defined architectural
forms and their interrelationships.

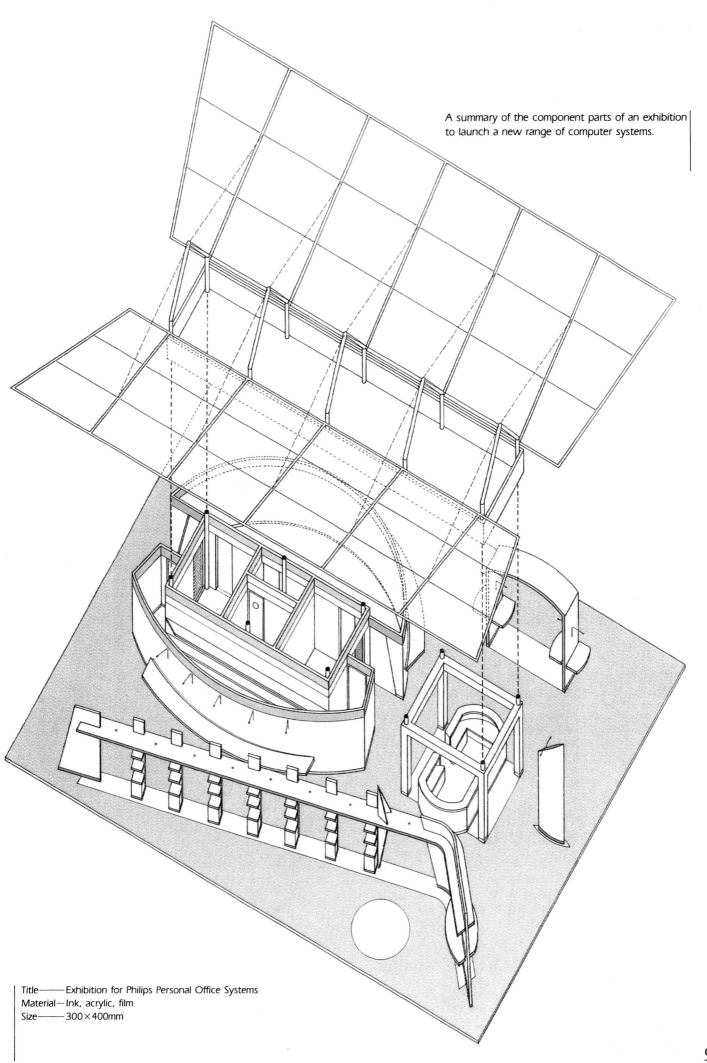

A summary of the component parts of an exhibition to launch a new range of computer systems.

Title——Exhibition for Philips Personal Office Systems
Material—Ink, acrylic, film
Size——300×400mm

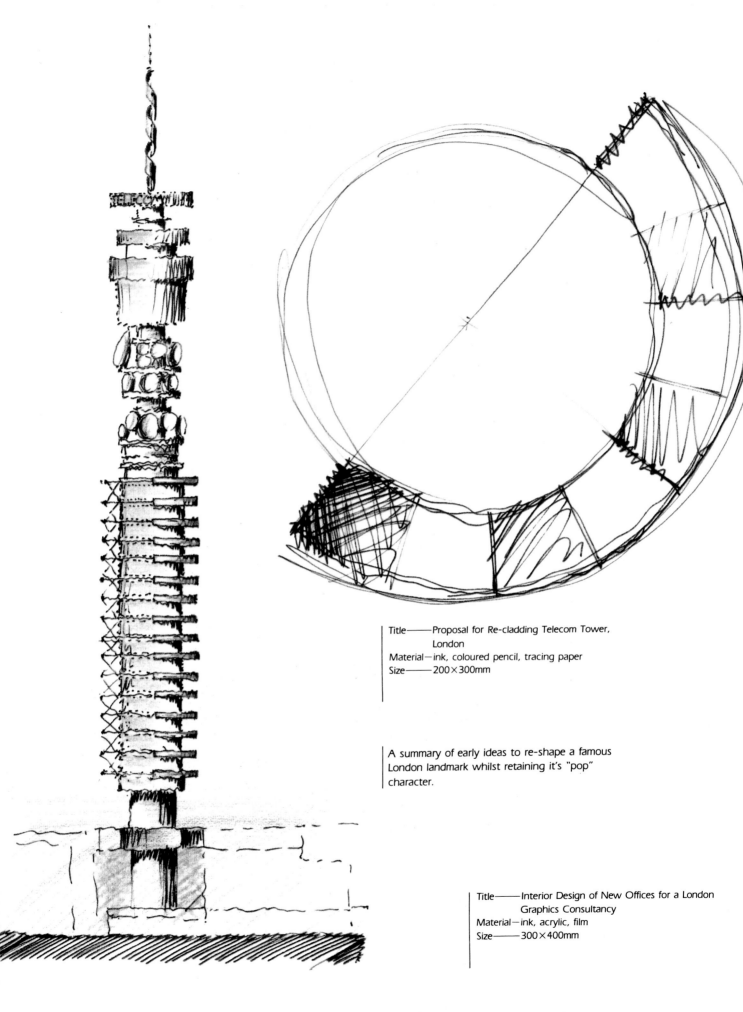

Title——Proposal for Re-cladding Telecom Tower,
          London
Material—ink, coloured pencil, tracing paper
Size——200×300mm

A summary of early ideas to re-shape a famous
London landmark whilst retaining it's "pop"
character.

Title——Interior Design of New Offices for a London
          Graphics Consultancy
Material—ink, acrylic, film
Size——300×400mm

A drawing to describe the geometry of free-standing
screens giving privacy and semi-privacy within an
old warehouse loft.

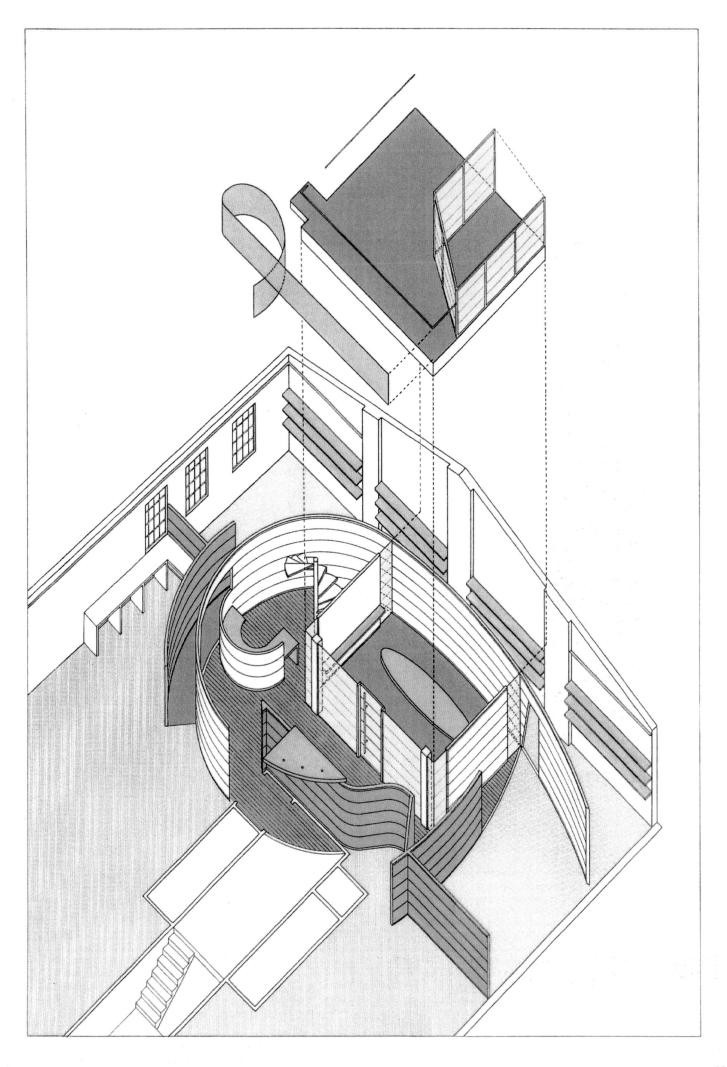

# Architekturbüro Bolles Wilson

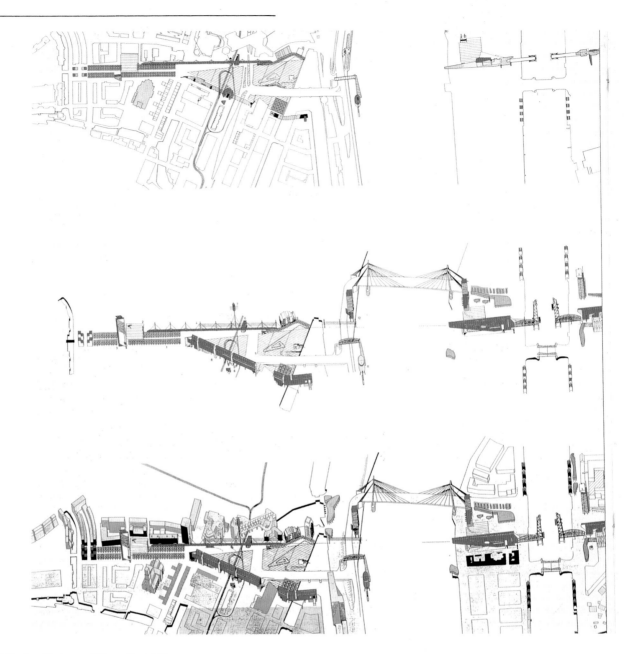

Title———Rotterdam Vectors - Railway Tunnel Site
Material—hand coloured xerox copies
Size———1000×1000mm(all)

Presentation of Urban Planning Commission for the City of Rotterdam.
Recently our explorations have focused on the discontinuous field of the contemporary city. This study for a 3 kilometer×50 meter strip across Rotterdam produced a language of autonomous floating buildings surrounded by smaller satelite infrastructure.
The plans explain the new elements to be inserted in the existing city pattern. The perspective shows a proposal for replacing the redundant "Hef" Lifting Bridge with two lifting restaurants.

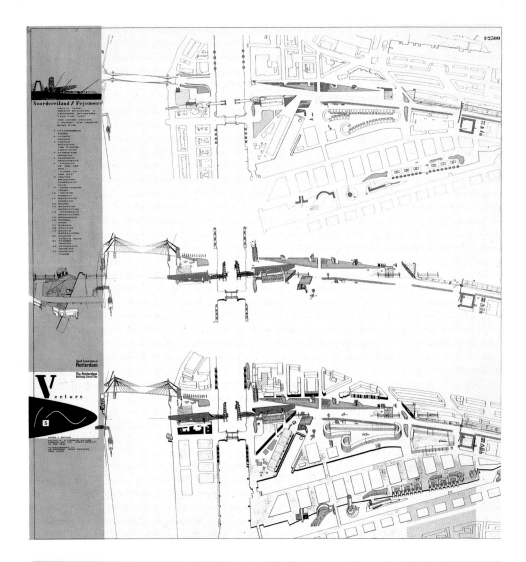

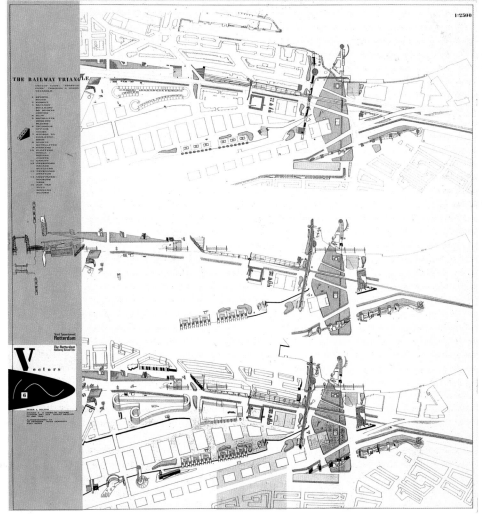

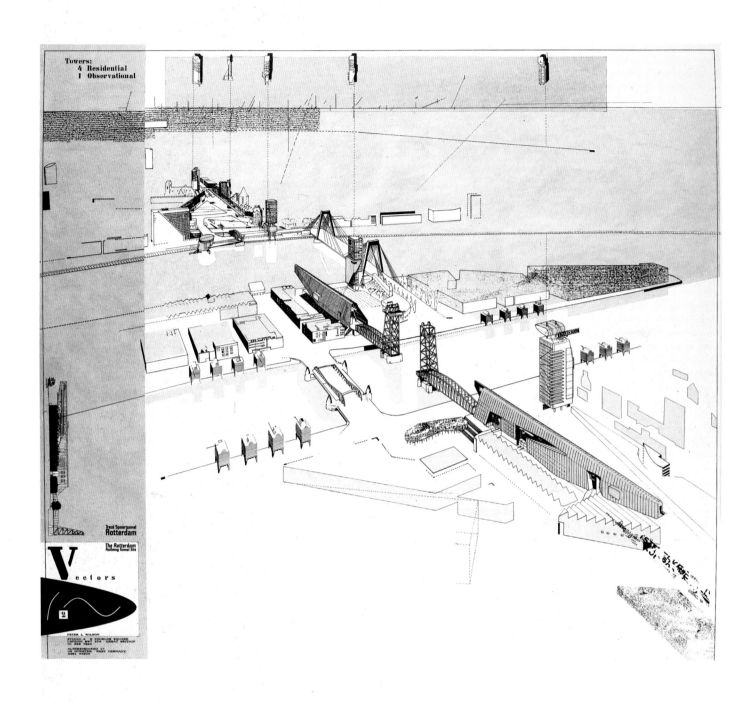

Towers:
4 Residential
1 Observational

Tracé Spoortunnel
Rotterdam

The Rotterdam
Railway Tunnel Site

**V**ectors
2

Title——————Rotterdam Vectors - Railway Tunnel Site
Material—hand coloured xerox copies
Size————1000×1000mm

The design which this sketch summarises won first
prize in an urban design competition. The colour
relates to the red brick quality of the city. The
perimeter bridge building and the surface of the
public space are animated by a scattering of
figurative elements. The sketch is a panorama of the
activated place.

Title——Mask of Liberty
Material—pencil, watercolour
Size——300×300mm

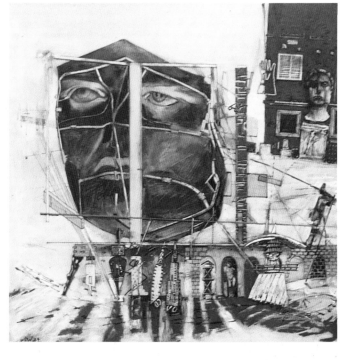

At this time our projects explored a language of contemporary figuration. Communicative elements, a scattered discontinuity of subplots stand mask - like and cast out of silent abstract architectural volumes.

Title——Domplatz, Hamburg
Material—pencil
Size——150×150mm

'DOMPLATZ' ~ HAMBURG ~ 1988 ~ P.L.WILSON

At this time I was pursuing an architecture stripped of convention, reduced to essential elements, timeless elements whose greatest affinity was with the earth.

Title——Public Convenience
Material—pencil, watercolour
Size——320×480mm

# Armstrong Associates

Title———Elementer Industrial Design H.Q. Building
Material—ink, film
Size———297×420mm

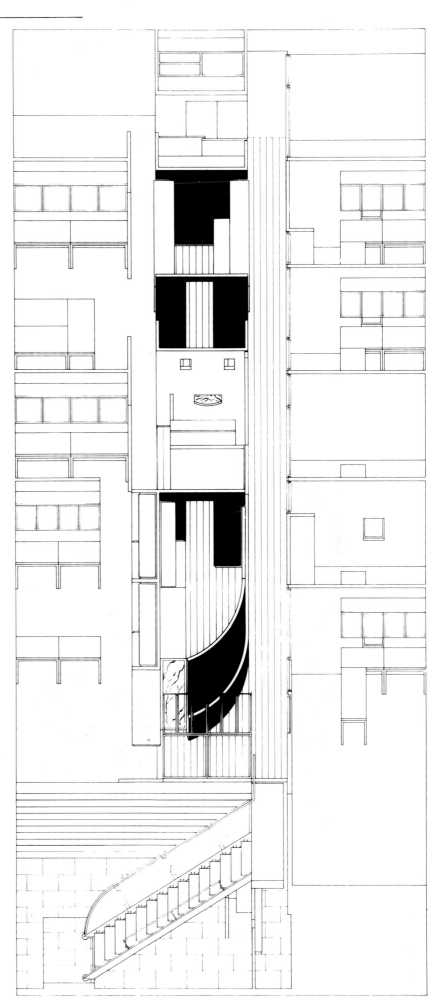

# Beevor Mull & Associates

Title———Orinoco
Material—Collage, paint, ink, card
Size———591×841mm

This drawing investigates the flattened internal
"landscape" of Orinoco, sound and vision. A built
"landscape" collaged textures, forms and signs. A
map through which the user is invited to "derive"
Recreating in two dimensions the real territory of
the completed project.

Title———The Beach
Material—modelling in string, resin etc., collage, paint,
ink, text
Size———297×420mm

These collages are part of a series of ten which
explore the analogy of the beach "(An endless space
swept daily by current forces leaving behind a
random flotsam of usable parts)" as the basis for an
architectural language which celebrates the capacity
of the user like a beachcomber to find their own
meaning and usefulness within a given place.

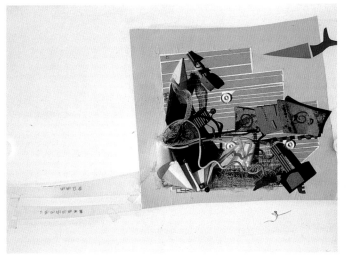

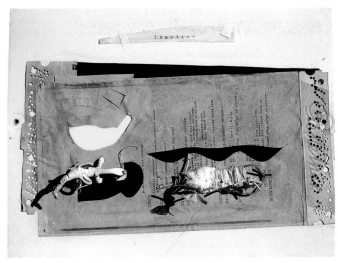

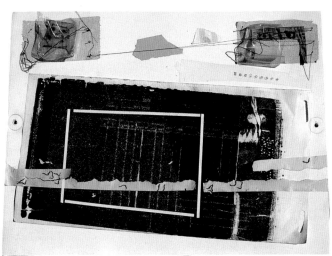

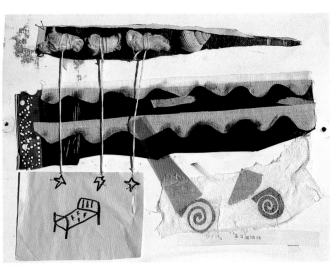

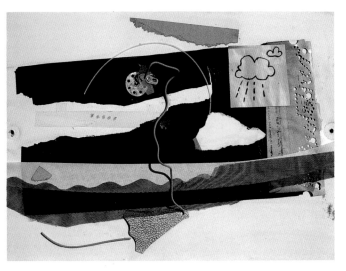

# Avci+Jurca

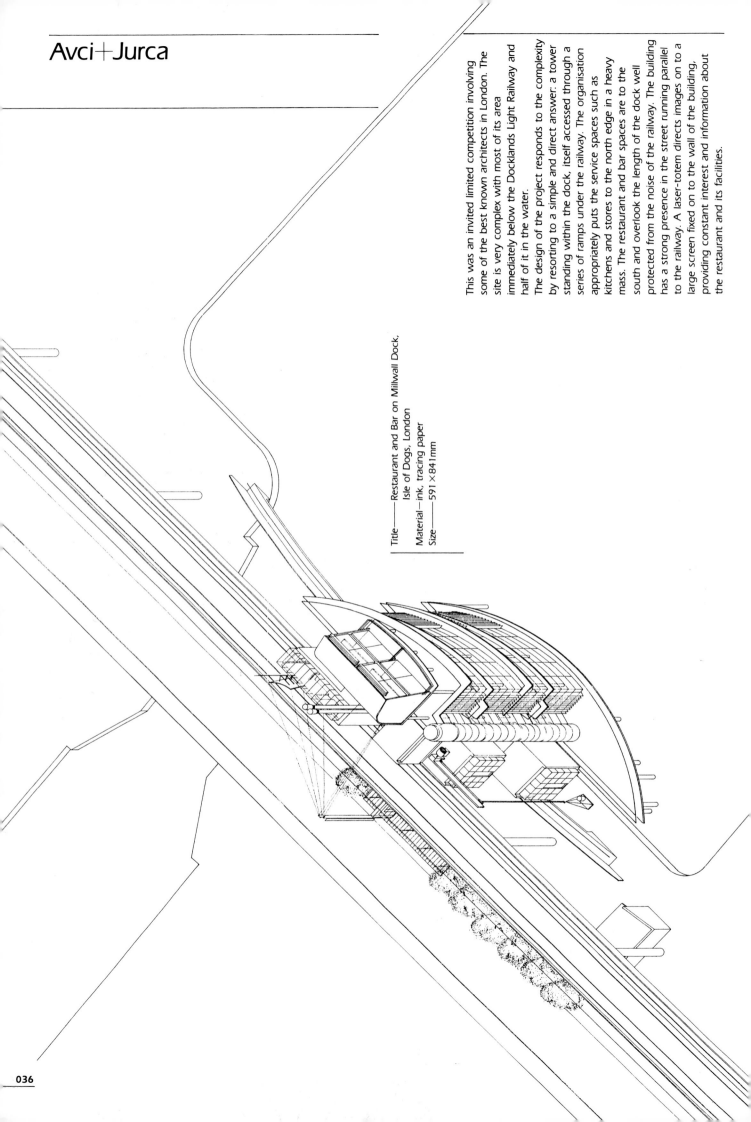

This was an invited limited competition involving some of the best known architects in London. The site is very complex with most of its area immediately below the Docklands Light Railway and half of it in the water.

The design of the project responds to the complexity by resorting to a simple and direct answer: a tower standing within the dock, itself accessed through a series of ramps under the railway. The organisation appropriately puts the service spaces such as kitchens and stores to the north edge in a heavy mass. The restaurant and bar spaces are to the south and overlook the length of the dock well protected from the noise of the railway. The building has a strong presence in the street running parallel to the railway. A laser-totem directs images on to a large screen fixed on to the wall of the building, providing constant interest and information about the restaurant and its facilities.

Title——Restaurant and Bar on Millwall Dock,
Isle of Dogs, London
Material—ink, tracing paper
Size——591×841mm

Title———Woodhead Manufacturing Co. "The Veil"
Material—ink, tracing paper
Size———591×841mm

"The Veil" is drawn in a manner suggesting a delicate mesh across the face of the existing 60's buildings fronting the main entrance to the factory. It is strictly a linear plane which defines a taut surface behind which a number of things go on. It anticipates a future (say in three years) when the whole site may be rationalised and the factory production lines placed in a linear extrusion behind the new facade stretching the whole length of the northern boundary. In it are set two "crystals", the

new main entrance to the offices and a security kiosk by the HGV entrance gates. These glass cases contrast with the rugged galvanised steel engineering aesthetic running throughout the scheme. Between the entrance and the gate is also a delicate translucent canopy giving shelter and scale to the wall.

The front area on Church Street is designed in the manner of a formal forecourt with two lines of semi-mature trees defining the edges. To the street the building and the court have an unambiguous relationship acting as a semi-public square along a busy route.

# Benedetti Renato Giovanni

Title———Channel Tunnel Train Station, Ludgate Hill,
                London.
Material—ink, paint, mylar(all)
Size———500×500mm(all)

RBAN GATEWAY LUDGATE CIRCUS CITY OF LONDON

MAIN ADDRESS WALL/SIGN ON LUDGATE CIRCUS & NEW BRIDGE STREET

NEW BRITISH

CUT AWAY VIEW FROM SOUTHBO

The new train station, planned beneath Ludgate Hill, will address the potential urban experience of a new gateway into London with the creation of a grand open space full of both light and movement. It will provide suburban commuters and international passengers coming in from the Channel Tunnel with a sense of arrival. It will replace a raised Victorian viaduct, and the rail lines will be positioned beneath Ludgate Hill to accommodate the 250 metre long platforms needed to take Channel Tunnel trains. Some of the brick fragments from the original viaduct will be retained in the hub of the new building.

The interior of the station will be barrel vaulted with some restaurants and other public facilities on the surface. The slope of Ludgate Hill has also been well utilised to allow easy connection to platforms.

'LONDON LINK" STATION

FORM

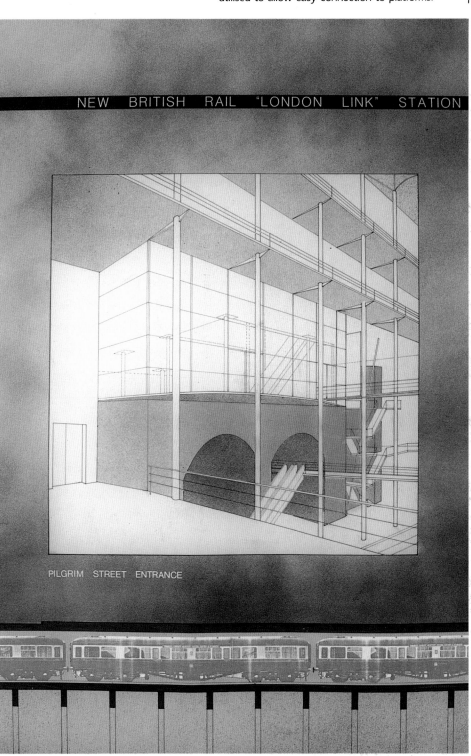

NEW BRITISH RAIL "LONDON LINK" STATION

PILGRIM STREET ENTRANCE

# Ben Kelly Design

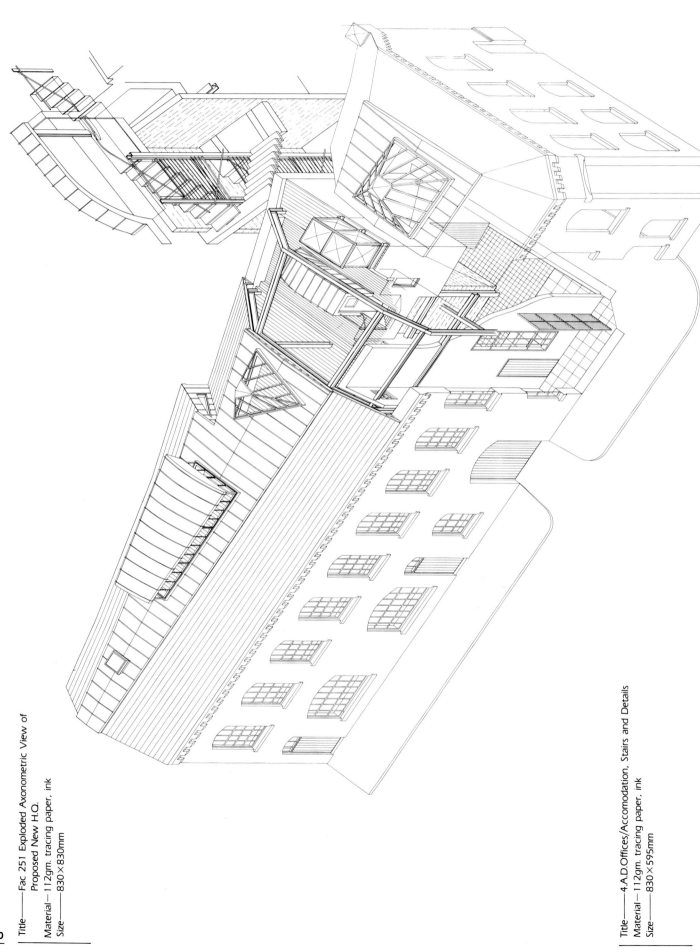

Title——Fac 251 Exploded Axonometric View of
        Proposed New H.Q.
Material— 112gm. tracing paper, ink
Size——830×830mm

Title——4.A.D.Offices/Accomodation, Stairs and Details
Material— 112gm. tracing paper, ink
Size——830×595mm

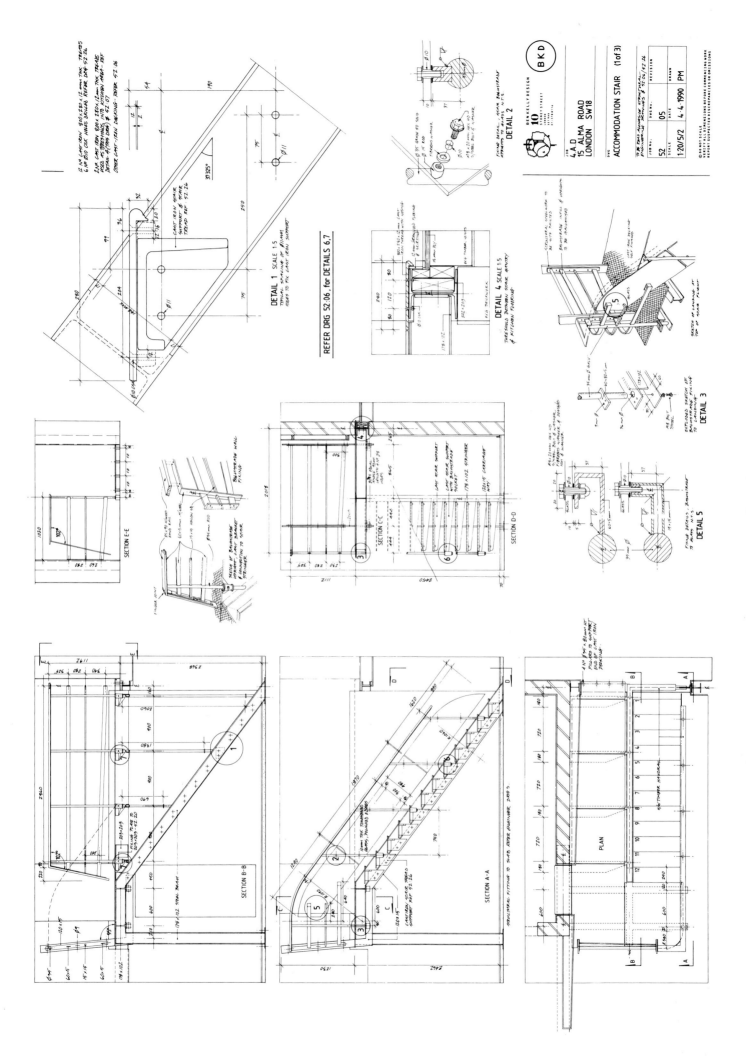

BKD

BEN KELLY DESIGN
10 STONEY STREET
LONDON
SE1

JOB 4 A.D
15 ALMA ROAD
LONDON SW18

ACCOMMODATION STAIR (1 of 3)

JOB No. 52
SCALE 05
DWG 120/5/2
DATE 4·4·1990
DRAWN PM

REVISION

DETAIL 2

DETAIL 1   SCALE 1:5

REFER DRG 52:06, for DETAILS 6,7

DETAIL 4   SCALE 1:5

DETAIL 3

DETAIL 5

SECTION E-E

SECTION C-C

SECTION D-D

SECTION B-B

SECTION A-A

PLAN

# Carlos Villanueva Brandt

Title———A Room
Material—oil pastel, collage, tracing paper
Size———290×290mm

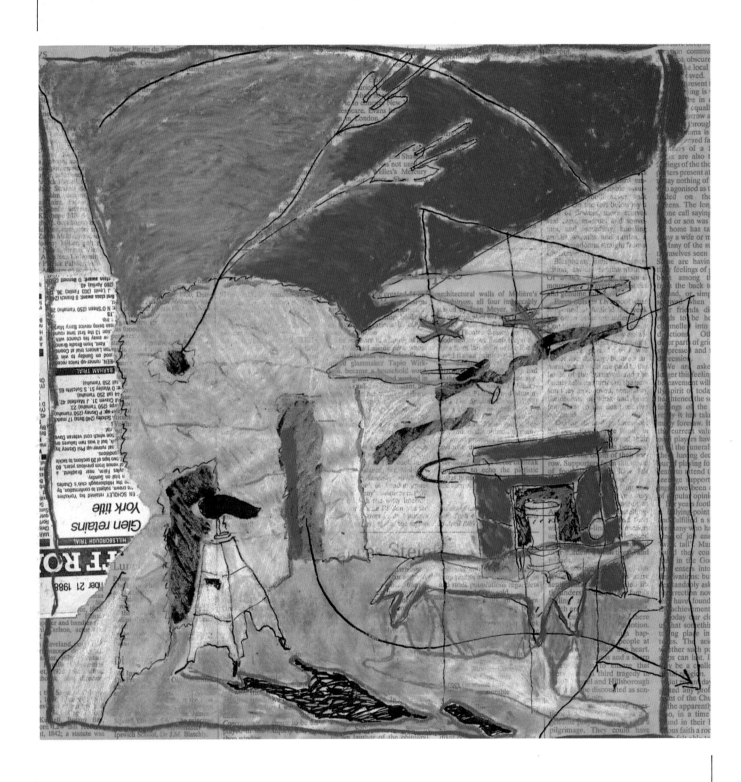

Drawn for an exhibition at 44 Ennismore Gardens, London, 1989. This drawing was the initial idea for the layout of the room and the objects contained within it. Along with another painting (which dealt with abstract possibilities of space within the canvas) and the built objects, it formed an integral part of the installation and became an ideogram for the spatial resolution.

Title——Heathrow Terminal 3
Material—oil, paper
Size——1450×1100mm

Painting for a N.A.T.O. exhibition at the ICA Boston.
The painting is one of a series of three that
investigated the possibilities of an information
terminal at Heathrow. Along with the construction
of composite objects the paintings can be regarded
as working drawings which are part of the process.
It is this "work in progress" analogy that gives life
to the works and allows them to become paintings
in their own right.

# Benson&Forsyth

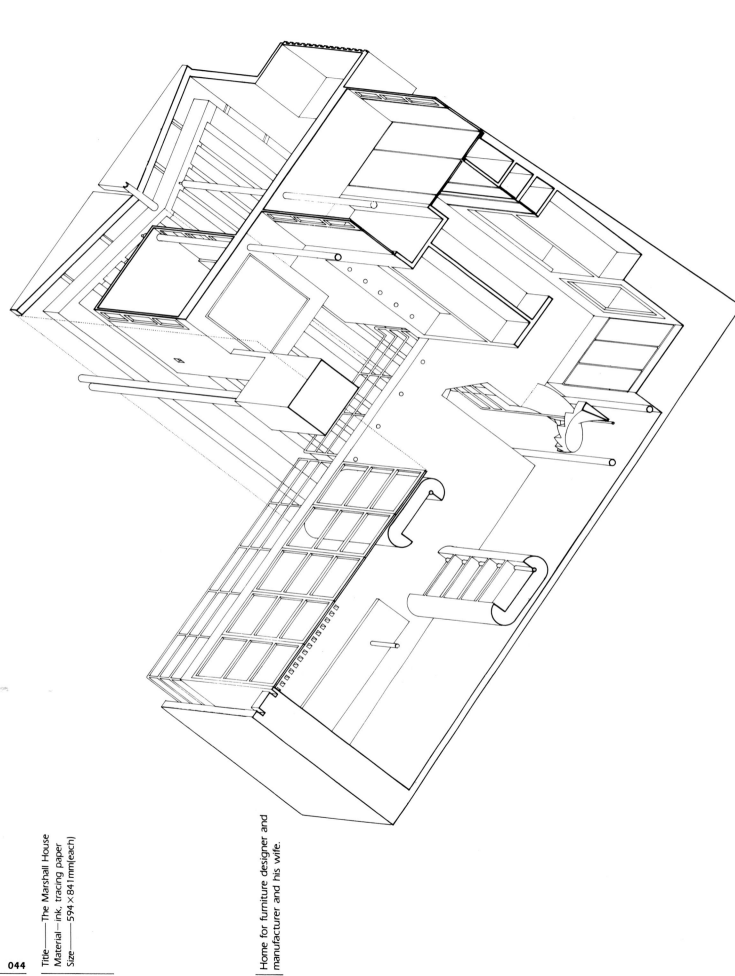

Title ——— The Marshall House
Material — ink, tracing paper
Size ——— 594 × 841 mm (each)

Home for furniture designer and manufacturer and his wife.

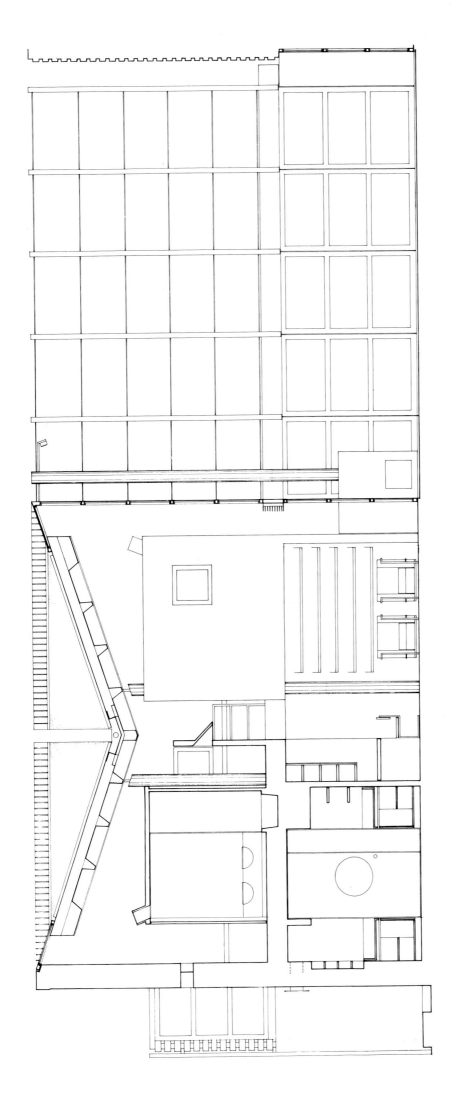

# Raoul Bunschoten

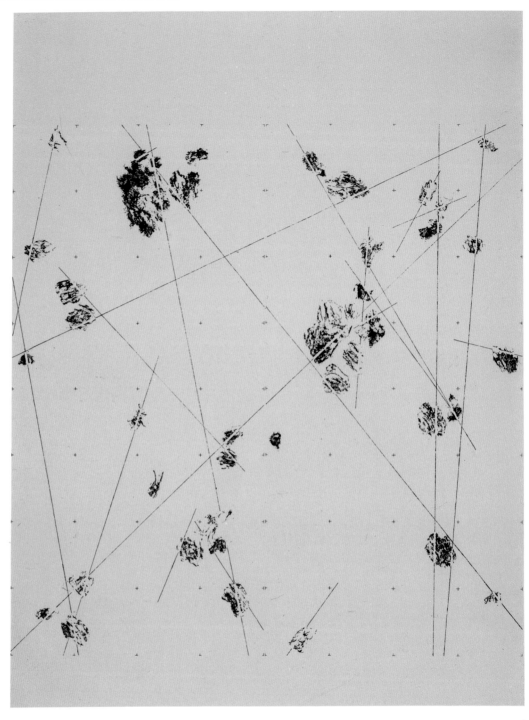

Title———"Apeiron" or Chaos Embodied,
        The Powergame, Berlin
Material—etching
Size———480×800mm

"Apeiron" or Chaos Embodied. "Apeiron" is the name of the boundless field full of boundaries in the middle of the city; a vast mass stretching outward apparently without end, boundless and timeless memory.

Its structure is Chaos, a yawning abyss, a formless void, with shattered debris of lived time and lived space which should be marked. "Apeiron" means in a truer sense also that which cannot be transversed from end to end.

The topographical outline of this field is formed through Unter den Linden, Otto Grotewohlstrasse, Viederleichnerstrasse, Kothenerstrasse, Landwehrkanal and the line along the Staatsbibliotek defined by the new building next to the former Potsdomer Guterbahnhof area.

Title——"Apeiron" or Chaos Embodied, Berlin
Material—etching
Size——950×1300mm

As with the Annunciation the "Apeiron" field is both
synopsis and "daeresis": it is centre of the city and
urban edge of two urban areas. The outline is
somewhat accidental as the shadow of a cloud
which changes the colour of the land momentarily.
A group or cluster of particles, elementary parts, is
strewn over the area, partly lifted from the ground.
Every particle is a place of origin, a womb
containing a quite particular space.
Together the particles form an Anaxagorean field of
spermatozoen, seeds of the urban space. Each is a
parasite (para-site), the earth is only carrier, it feeds
only the consciousness and is no ground to build.
The parasite is new land, new ground which is cut
anew by streets, it opens itself spatially. An
architectural field emerges.

# Campbell Zogolovitch Wilkinson & Gough Architects

Title——Radio City - Motorway View of Development
Material—ink, tracing paper
Size——594×841mm

Title——Radio City - Courtyard High Space
Material—ink, pencil render, tracing paper
Size——594×841mm

The acutely triangular, virtually landlocked, site of Radio City at White City is more than half underneath the junction of two motorways. Clearly a silk purse out of a sow's ear project, visions soon locked on to the smoggy blue backdrop of freeway city; this would be a prime site in LA. Accordingly, the approach beneath the motorway becomes a swathe cut for a flash flood river bed through a dynamically irrigated rain forest of glossy green caryatids.

The building itself (actually a twentieth-century "chambers") had to appear to be more of a piece of engineering than the flyover.

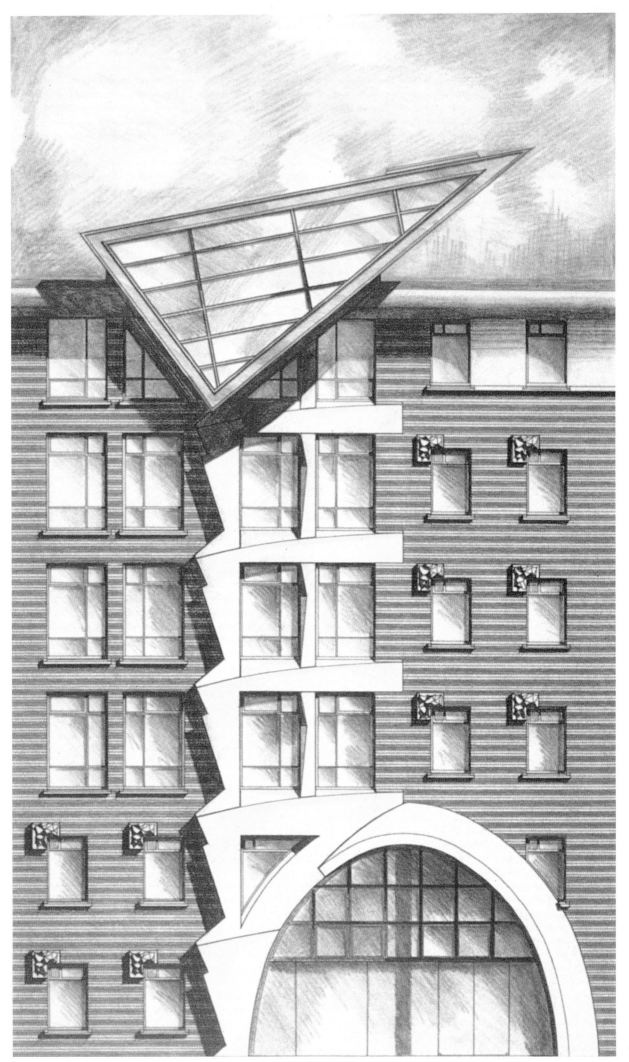

# Nick Coombe

Title———The ICA Foyer
Material—linocut
Size———120×180mm

A new bookshop for the existing foyer is in the form of a wall of cupboards along one side. At night when closed, the bookshop folds protectively like an armadillo inside itself, while evening events are staged.

Title——The Oyster Club
Material—linocut
Size——80×120mm/120×80mm

A London nightclub devised and constructed for a
T.V.show of the same name.

Proposal for the Living Room that may become a sanctuary (a cave) safe from the violent city beyond.

Title——Own Flat
Material—collage, coloured ink
Size——270×400mm

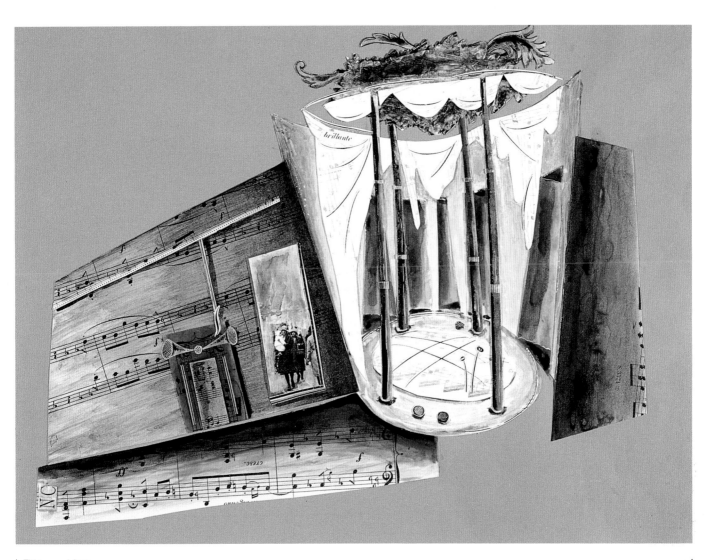

Title————Vivre
Material—collage
Size————300×450mm

Idea collages for areas of a new fashion store in Yokohama Japan. Based on a brief written by Hiroshi Shioi entitled "The European City of the Near Future".

# D'Soto '88 Design Group

Imagine a space. A musty dormant relic of an older machine age, suddenly and brutally shocked into being. A new life force is here. Jazz music, a restless urge. Jazz, a multi-headed hybrid. The space responds, mutates. The very fabric of the architecture changes. Old, rough wood is kissed and embraced by gleaming new steel. New walls create a new sense of scale. It becomes a giant heart, pulsing with new life. All is red, a deep blood red. Floor, walls, ceiling all one colour. Rhythm, light, the old and the new, the cold and the warm. All is here. The space becomes an enigma, a fusion of yesterday and tomorrow to create today.

Title———— A Jazz Club, South London
Material—tracing paper, pencil, ink, photocopier
Size———— Entirely variable

Title———A Jazz Club, South London
Material—tracing paper, ink, blue pencil
Size————595×420mm

Thoughts, impulses, scratches and collages are but the start of the imaginative process. They are symbols, a visual code to facilitate the creative exchange of information. The type and quality of the marks one makes are as varied as their functions. When a concensus is reached, and a uniform vision is shared, the line itself mutates. What was once a slash of pencil lead expressing enthusiasm, dynamism and vigour, becomes a regulated and controlled black line denoting control, resolve and consideration. Clear explanation becomes a necessity. Naturally, every line has its time and place.

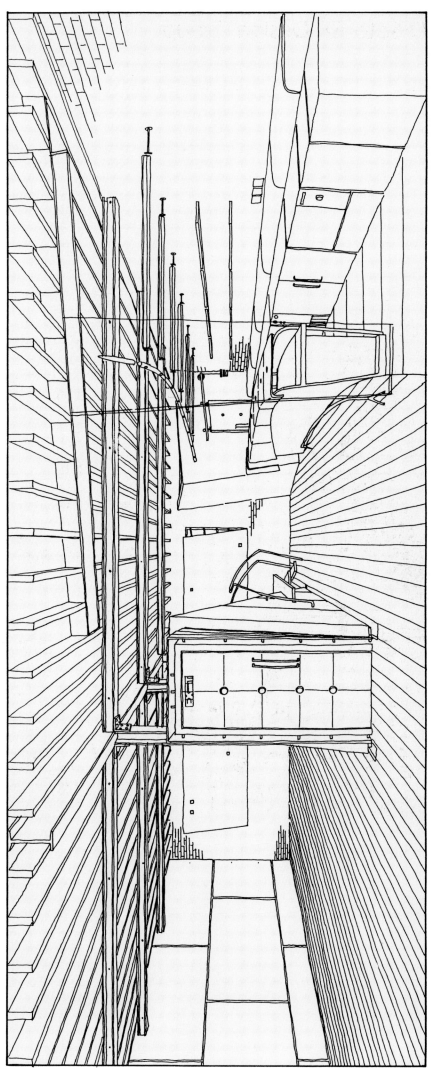

# Guy Comely

Title——Langans Restaurant
Material—pencil, gouache, charcoal
Size——1200×820mm

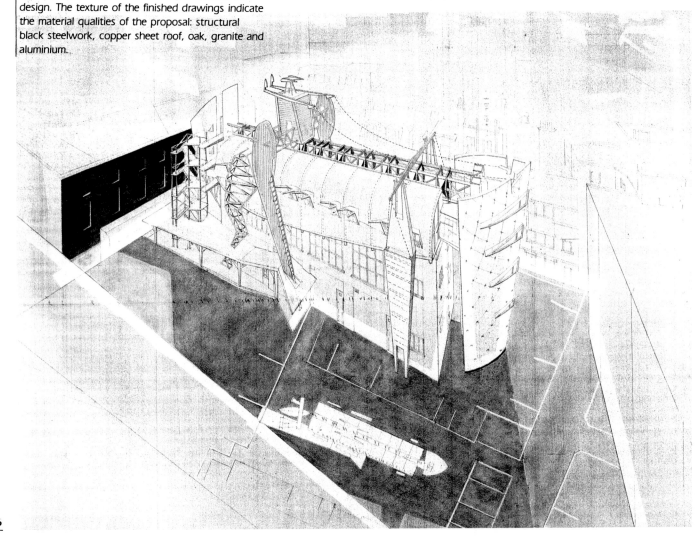

This proposal for a new restaurant in London's St.James implies an intense layered urban condition since it is sited straddling an exisiting electrical substation. The building is figurative in concept representing a horse and rider, restaurant and restauranteur. The body of the horse accommodates a dining chamber, the head the kitchen and entrance and the tail the exit and cloakrooms. The riding figure with reins accommodates a small rest room with hammock for the restauranteur and is accessed along the backbone from which the dining chamber is hung. The limbs of the animal have become structural scaffolding and torsion restraints. The craft of making these drawings informed the design. The texture of the finished drawings indicate the material qualities of the proposal: structural black steelwork, copper sheet roof, oak, granite and aluminium.

Title——Langans Restaurant
Material—pencil, gouache, charcoal
Size——820×600mm

# David Chipperfield Architects

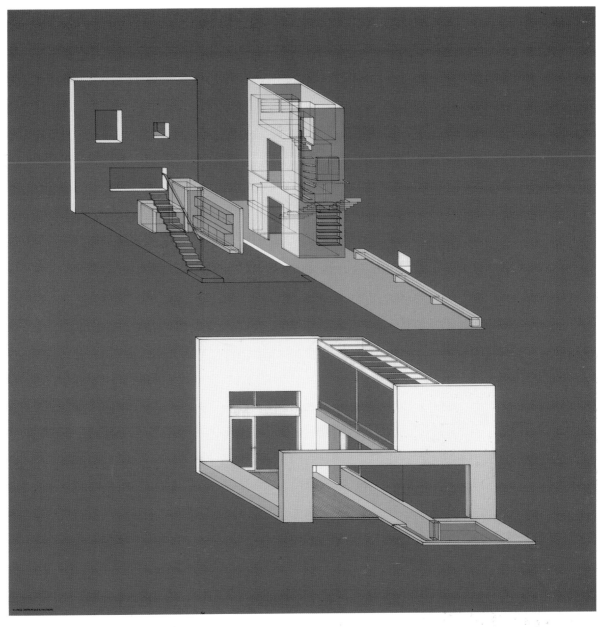

Title———Nick Knight Residence
Material—oil, linen canvas, negative shadow projection:
       ink, drafting film
Size———560×560mm, 560×560mm

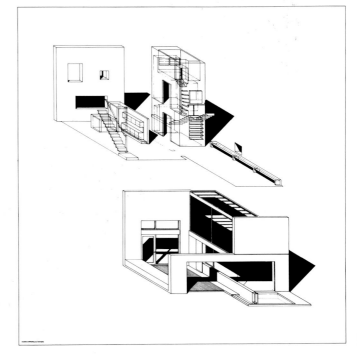

Drawings show the elemental composition of the
plan; the arch, the tower, the stairs. The plan is a
consequence of positioning these pieces.

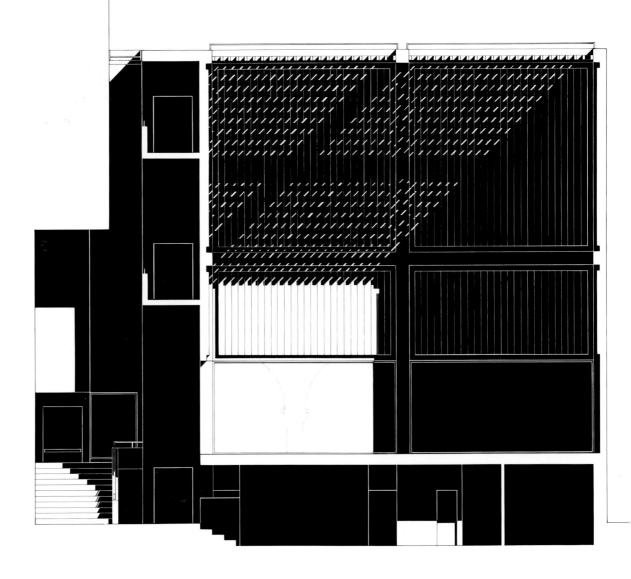

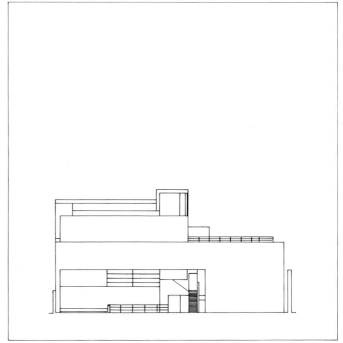

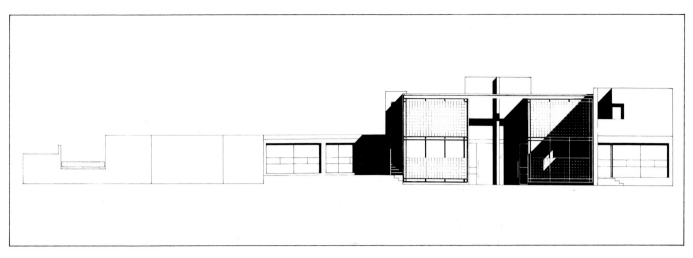

Title———First Church of Christ, Scientist
Material—ink, drafting film
Size———594×841mm

Title———Agar Grove Studios
Material—shadow projection: ink, drafting film
Size———594×594mm

The project involves the design of a prime 15 metre
cube space, animated only by light. This drawing
tries to communicate the effect of that light.

Title———Series - Recent Projects - Elevations
Material—ink, drafting film
Size———594×841mm

Drawing emphasises abstract composition of
elevation and shadowing clarifies the three
dimensional qualities.

Current projects all drawn at a comparative size.

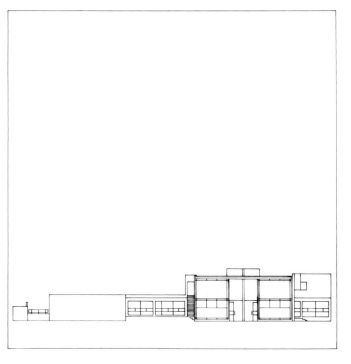

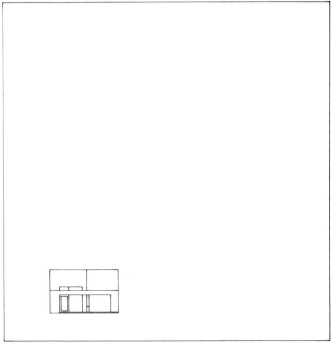

# Din Associates

Title——"HYPE", London
Material—colour pencil, oil pastels, tracing paper
Size——297×420mm

Due to open in the King's Road, Chelsea in February 1991, Hype DF is a 1,200 sq.metre complex which is a breakthrough in modern day retailing. Fashion designers from around the world will be present in retail sections to target the 18-35 age group. The inner space will be interactive with audio visual technology, fashion shows on suspended catwalks and a performance platform for young bands and artists. This flag ship is the first phase of a five-year program that will extend into the major capitals of the world.

Title——"HYPE", London
Material—colour pencil, oil pastels, tracing paper
Size——297×420mm

Title——"HYPE", London
Material—colour pencil
Size——297×420mm

# David Marks Julia Barfield
# Architects

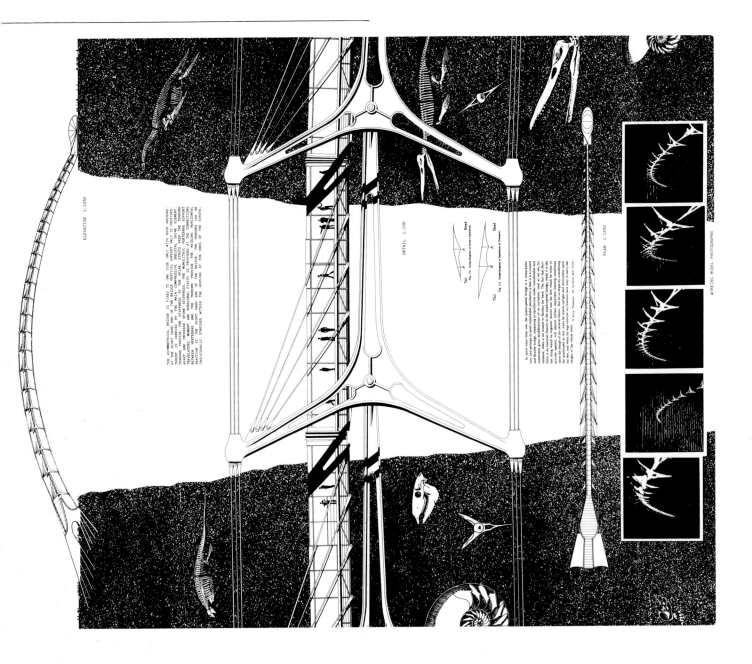

Title——Bridge of the Future
Material—ink, film, applied photocopy images
Size——600×850mm

Selected from one hundred entries - judges' comments: this was the one we felt best expressed the theme of an "image of the bridge of the future". The graphical image is striking with the derivations of the idea clearly expressed. The brief referred to the world of nature and the relationship between nature and structure are explored well. The bridge would be a joy to behold and a pleasure to walk over.

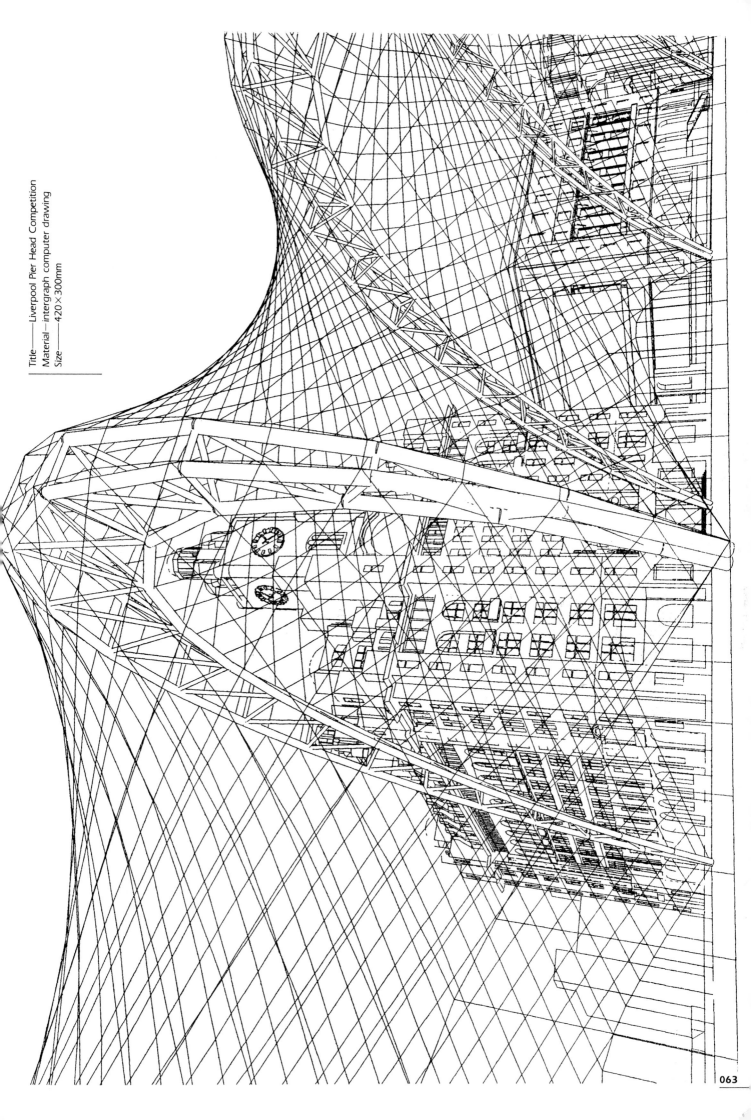

Title————Liverpool Pier Head Competition
Material—intergraph computer drawing
Size————420×300mm

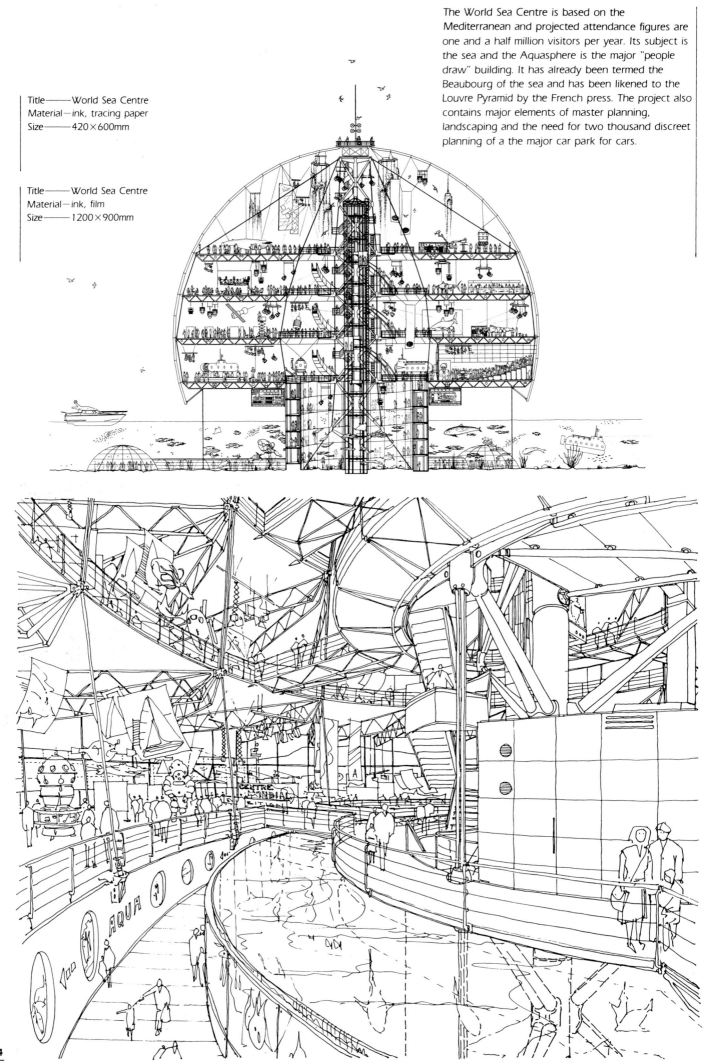

The World Sea Centre is based on the Mediterranean and projected attendance figures are one and a half million visitors per year. Its subject is the sea and the Aquasphere is the major "people draw" building. It has already been termed the Beaubourg of the sea and has been likened to the Louvre Pyramid by the French press. The project also contains major elements of master planning, landscaping and the need for two thousand discreet planning of a the major car park for cars.

Title———World Sea Centre
Material—ink, tracing paper
Size———420×600mm

Title———World Sea Centre
Material—ink, film
Size———1200×900mm

# Catherine'Du Toit

Title———Mecca Store — High Street Exchanges
Material—mixed media, mylar
Size———549×841mm

A project exploring and exploiting the nature of research and the concepts of factory farming. It is a place for the germination and maturing of ideas. The complex is comprised of a factory floor, test-ring and show-ring, all linked by electronic filters and screens. The station seeks, via its choreography, to provide researchers with a mouthpiece, and to increase the amount of expertise able to be drawn from other fields.

The section was developed as part of a study of the factory floor and potting sheds. (For those individual scientists). The emergent technology for constructing the architecture was based on the principles found in the biological world — vital services become an integral part of the structural system, the different elements being grafted together.

Ultimately the development of the station becomes inextricably bonded with the nature of the research it conducts.

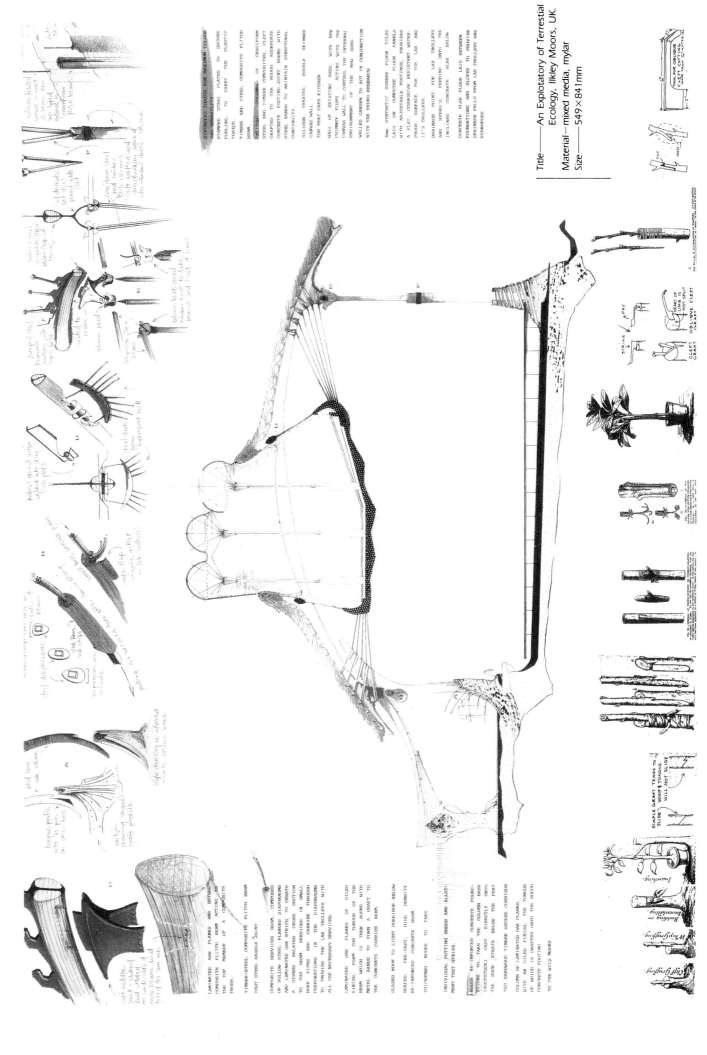

Title——An Explotatory of Terrestial
Ecology, Ilkley Moors, UK.
Material——mixed media, mylar
Size——549×841mm

# Edward Cullinan Architects

Title——House in Walled Garden, Oakley House,
         Bedfordshire
Material—colour ink
Size——210×297mm

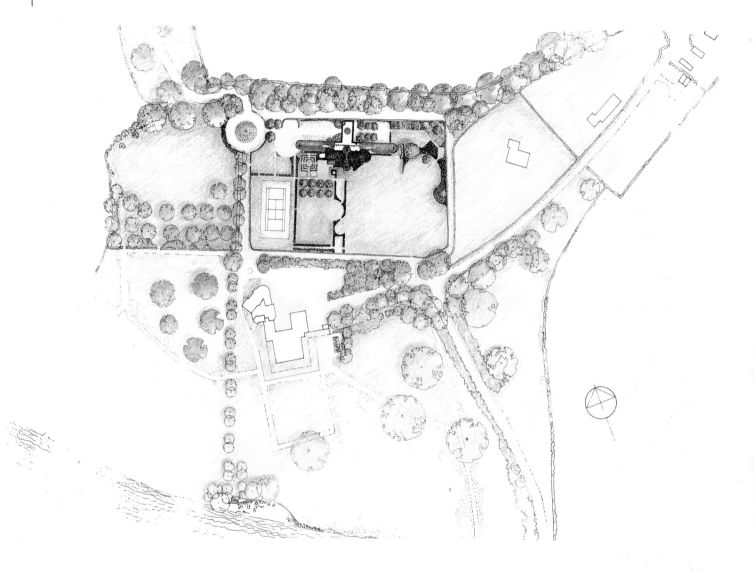

Set within an existing historic walled garden, this
private house follows the line of existing linear south
facing greenhouses. It has a heavy north wall of a
local pale cream stone called church framed in red
brick and a predominantly glazed south wall
protected with planting boxes and trailing wisteria.
The internal arrangement of rooms, some of which
extend into the garden, generate divisions within the
garden forming parterres to the south of the house
for tennis, a formal garden, an orchard and a large
lawned area. Similarly, the north wall defines
between it and the existing garden wall a forecourt,
a covered porch, parking area and a herb garden.
The roof of the house is treated as a terraced
garden in which two main bedrooms, the hall
lantern and the study stand as pavillion. The upper
garden is connected by hedged ramps to the
garden.

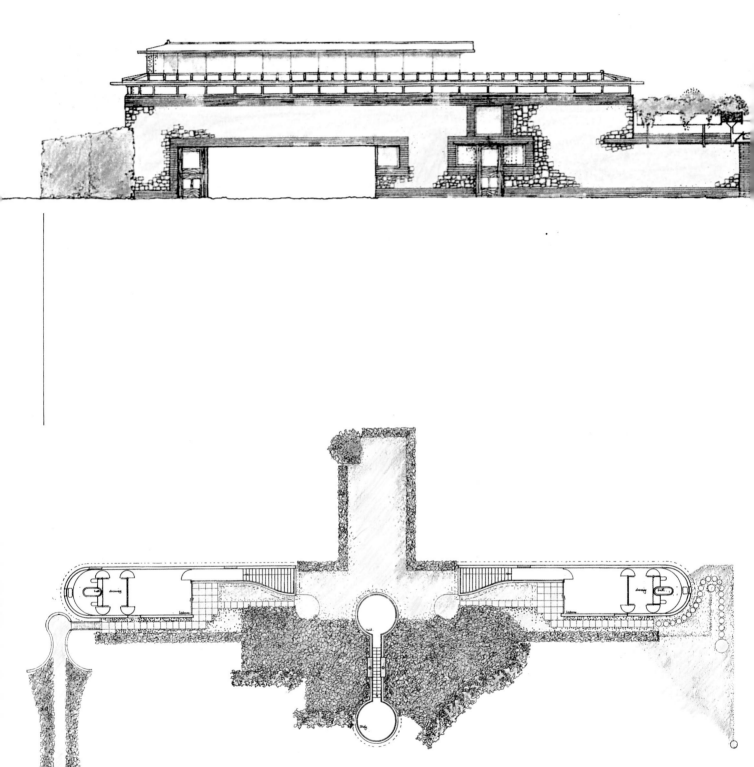

Title———House in Walled Garden, Oakley House, Bedfordshire
Material—colour ink
Size———210×297mm

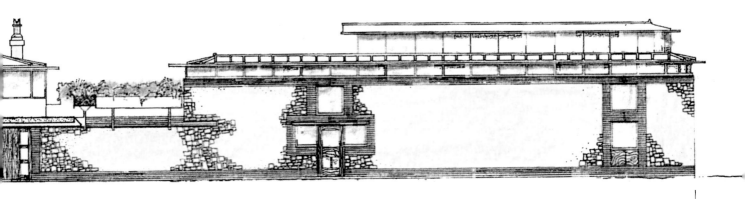

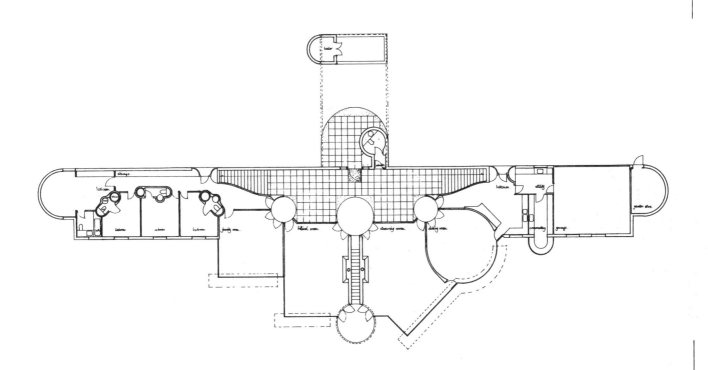

# Fisher Park Limited

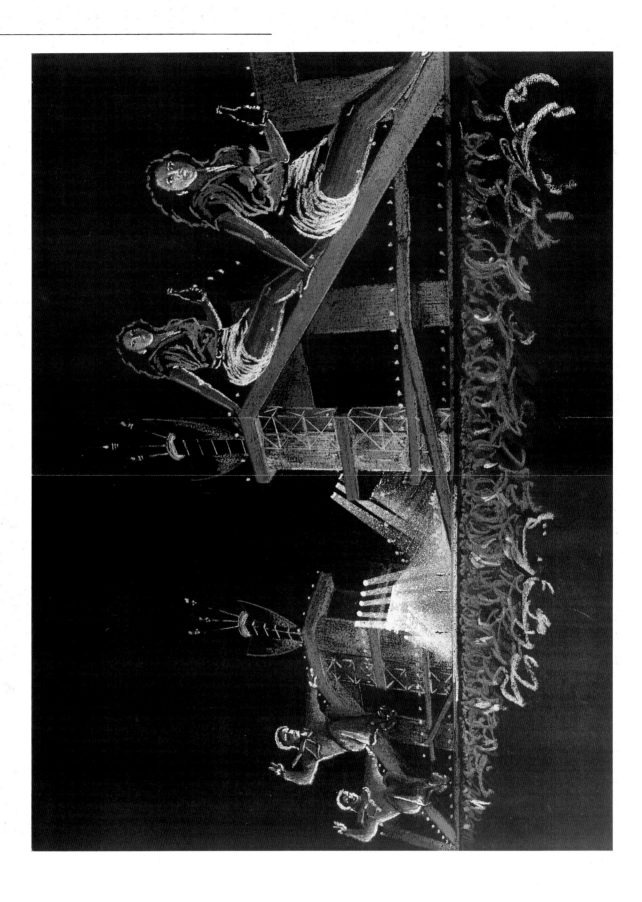

Title———Stage Set Design for the Rolling Stones
"Steel Wheels" U.S.Tour

Material—chalk, paper

Size———405×540mm

Title——Proposed Multi-media
 Concert by Jean-Michel
 Jarre in Shinjuku, Tokyo
Material—acrylic, card
Size——730×910mm

Title———Stage Set Design for the
　　　　Rolling Stones "Steel Wheels"
　　　　U.S.Tour
Material—india ink, watercolour, paper
Size———555×370mm

# William Firebrace

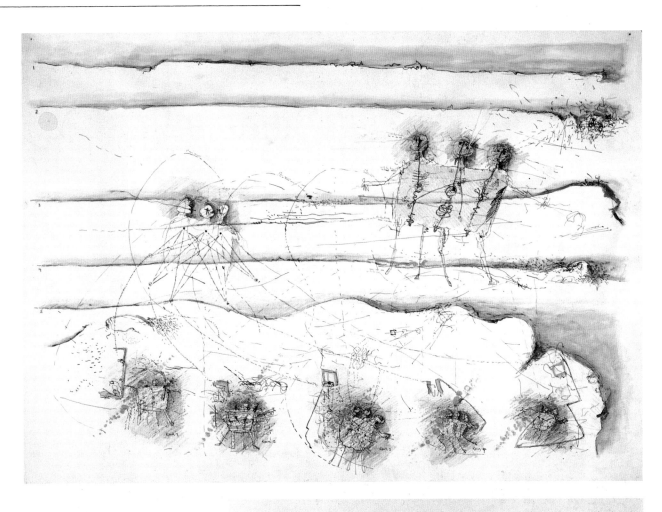

Title———The Anatomical Landscape
Material—ink, watercolour, pencil
Size———Slides 1 and 4, 210×290mm
        Slides 2 and 3, 600×840mm

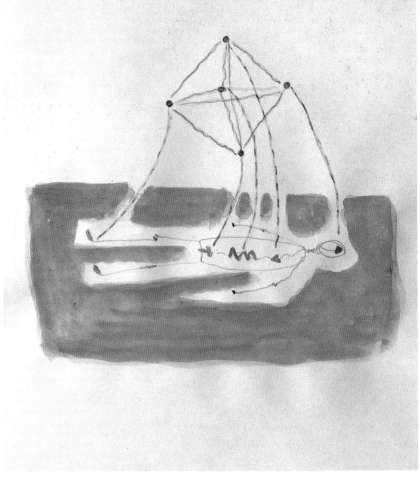

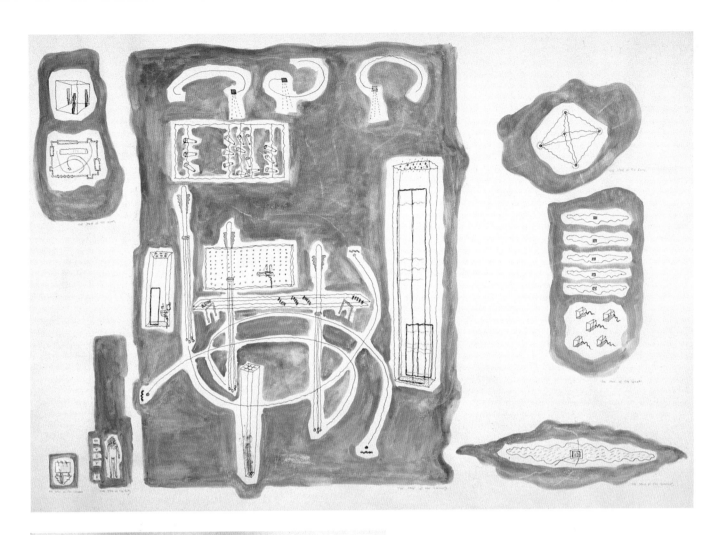

Out in the countryside three armies fight a battle. The bodies of those who perish are buried under the fields. (1)The borders of the battle are marked with five farms. A horizontal human figure lies on the ground and marks the five points with its organs. (2)A triple figure wanders across the ground and stops at each farm. (3)Beside each farm is a room of metal lined with silk within a wood. Set in the walls are an entrance, a w.c., a wine store and three cupboards containing a wheelchair. These chairs are on tracks and run to three objects in the room; a shaft filled with fire, a table, and a device to control sunlight. All the furniture is oversized, unusable. The wine is consumed and returned to the land via the w.c. (4)The red room and the chairs running on their tracks. The rooms are removed until only floors remain. The triple movement patterns are repeated five times over, their tracks. After a period of time the rooms are removed; only their floors remain. The triple movement patterns, repeated five times over, lie abandoned in the woods, remnants of a vanished anatomy.

# Pedro Guedes

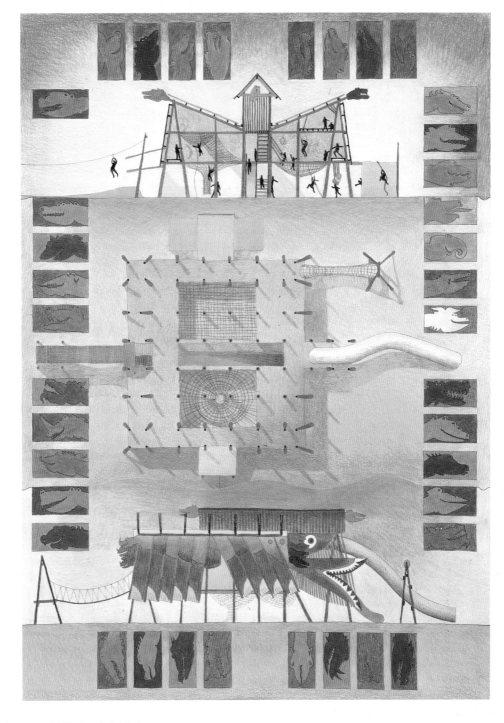

Title———Children's Playground, Windsor Safari Park
Material—pencil, crayon
Size———420×300mm

I've always wanted to build a building with lots of columns - a hypostyle hall. The columns are less than two metres apart and are made of tree trunks. The space inside is three storeyes high with double volumes filled with netting. The building is a large monster with gargoyles which I cut and stained myself. It is a place to feel danger safely.

The border of the picture is made up of the shapes of gargoyles. The style of the drawing comes from the child within me superimposed on a plan section and elevation from which the building was constructed.

Title———Kitchen
Material—watercolour, crayon, ingres paper
Size———840×620mm

The elevation of a self-made kitchen, the furniture of which was made from Edwardian and Victorian bits and pieces. Two grilles above the cooking hobs represent the temple of fire. The centrepiece is a house for drying dishes. The place on the right is a granary. Above it on the left is a night sky that also gives way to dawn. All items were rescued from oblivion. The drawings began before the reality and finished after it. The portraits sometimes give me ideas that I would not otherwise have thought of.

# Zaha Hadid

Title —— 1. Middle buildings
    2. Corner buildings(Hamburg, Hafenstrasse)
Material—acrylic paint, cartridge paper, cotton
Size —— 1. 1000×1190mm
    2. 1000×1760mm

A slab building is proposed on the acute corner of Bernard Nochstrasse and Hafenstrasse that will open its face to the riverfront. It will be a collation of two residential layers followed by two commercial layers which will be reached via the public space on the first two levels. Each floor creates a different entry space from the elevator. A sky lobby separates the offices from the penthouse above. Each floor can have an outdoor terrace by the use of sliding sections of glass curtained walls.

Title———The Melting Panton
Material—acrylic paint, cartridge paper, cotton
Size———1200×2700mm

Commemorating the twentieth. anniversary of the
Panton Chair, designed in 1969 by Verner Panton
for Vitra.

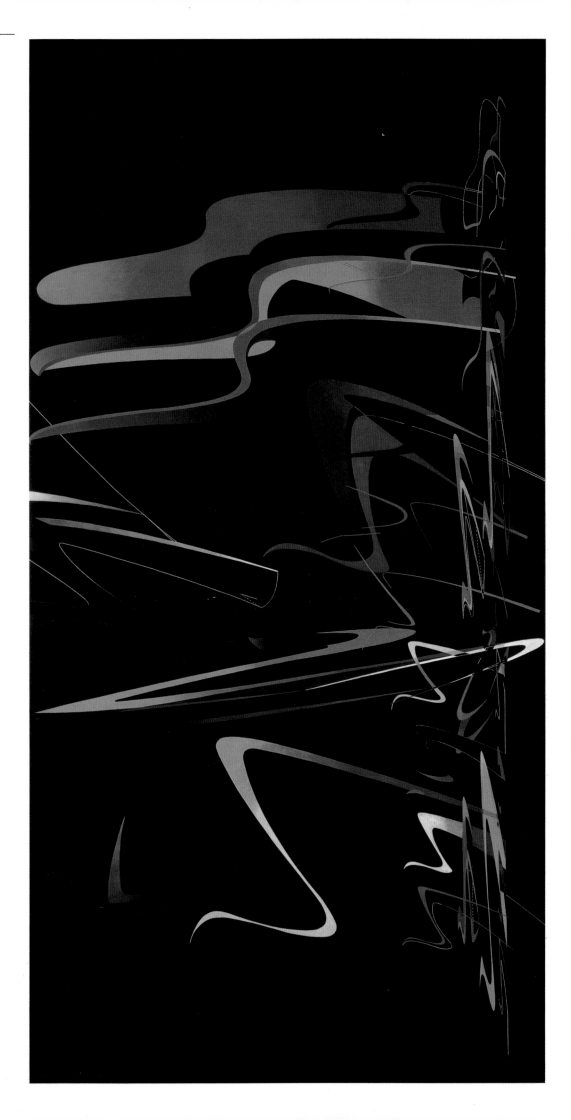

Title———Night and Day, Grand Buildings
　　　　　Competition painting
Material—acrylic paint, cartridge paper, linen
Size———700×2500mm(each)

Trafalgar Square has recently become nothing more than a simple traffic island. Nearby on Northumberland Street a slab of offices has been built with a series of towers and a shopping concourse. Each tower can be utilised by a single or a group of companies which can share general services. The towers give off a different aura when viewed from the vantage point of the Strand or

Northumberland Avenue. A present car-parking area with a capacity of fifty cars could be increased upon in the future. The ramp that leads from the shopping concourse curves around the structure until it arrives on the roof of the terrace. Spectacular new views of the Trafalgar Square traffic island are now possible.

# Eva Jiricna Architects

Title———Underground Station at Hillingdon
Material—photographic reproduction, added colour
Size———594×841mm

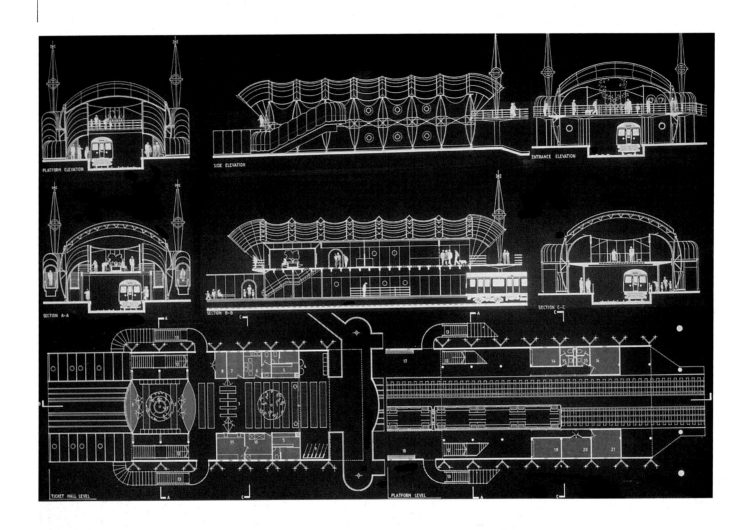

The location of the station was carefully chosen to allow existing services to continue during construction, and to prevent delays in the construction of the new A40 road. Access is provided by a horizontal bridge, a ramp/bridge and a ramp from the car park. The ticket hall and waiting room are at deck level and private accommodation in the form of prefabricated cabins is provided on either side of the ticket hall. Ancillary accommodation is also provided beneath the station deck. Access from the station deck to the platforms is by staircase and escalator.

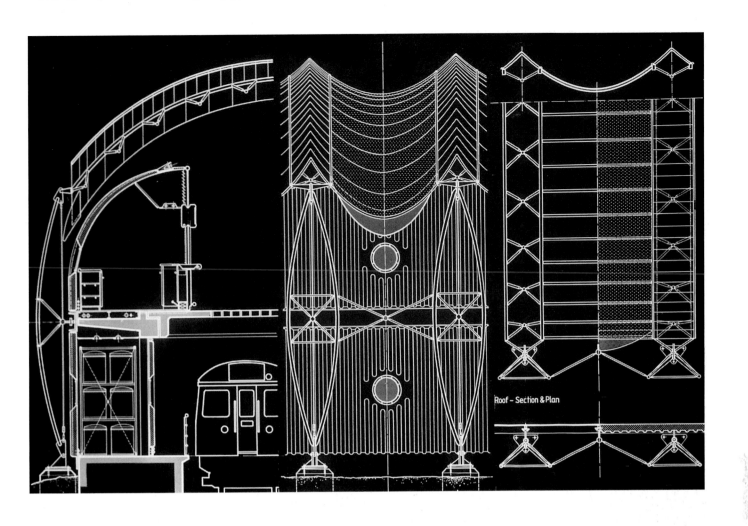

Roof – Section & Plan

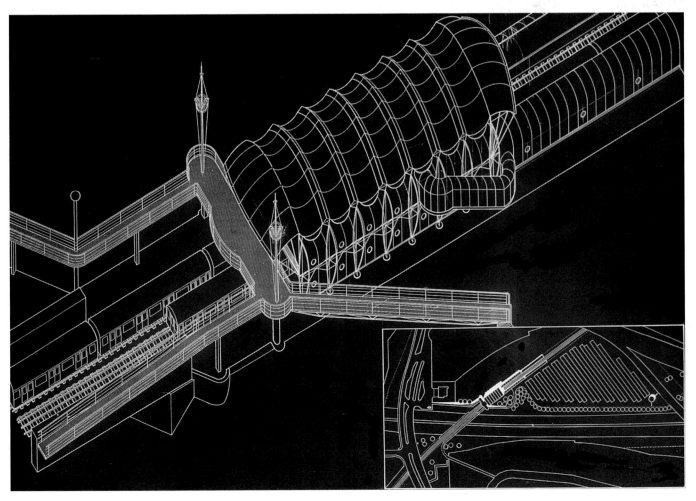

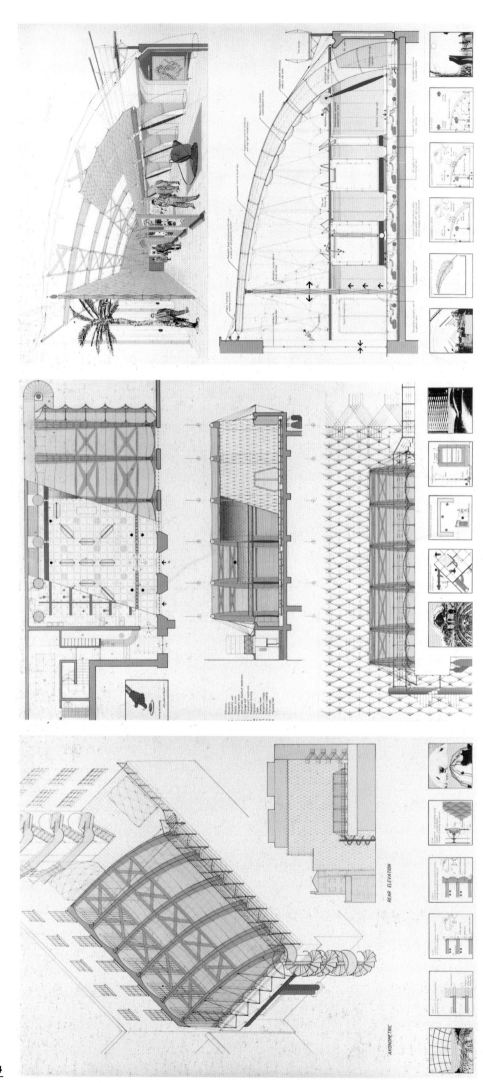

Title——— RIBA Gallery Extension Competition

Material— photographic reproduction, added colour

Size ———594×841mm

The gallery is an extension to the Florence Hall and is an enclosed gallery of 160sq. metres in area. Consideration has been given to the design to enable construction to go ahead without disruption. The gallery includes facilities to allow diffused daylight into the area, but can be changed to an artificially light controlled space with the use of a roller blind and a vertical inflatable wall.

# Andrew Holmes

Title———Tanks
Material—colour pencil, cartridge paper
Size———790×530mm

Drawing of milk storage tanks with gantry and tower.

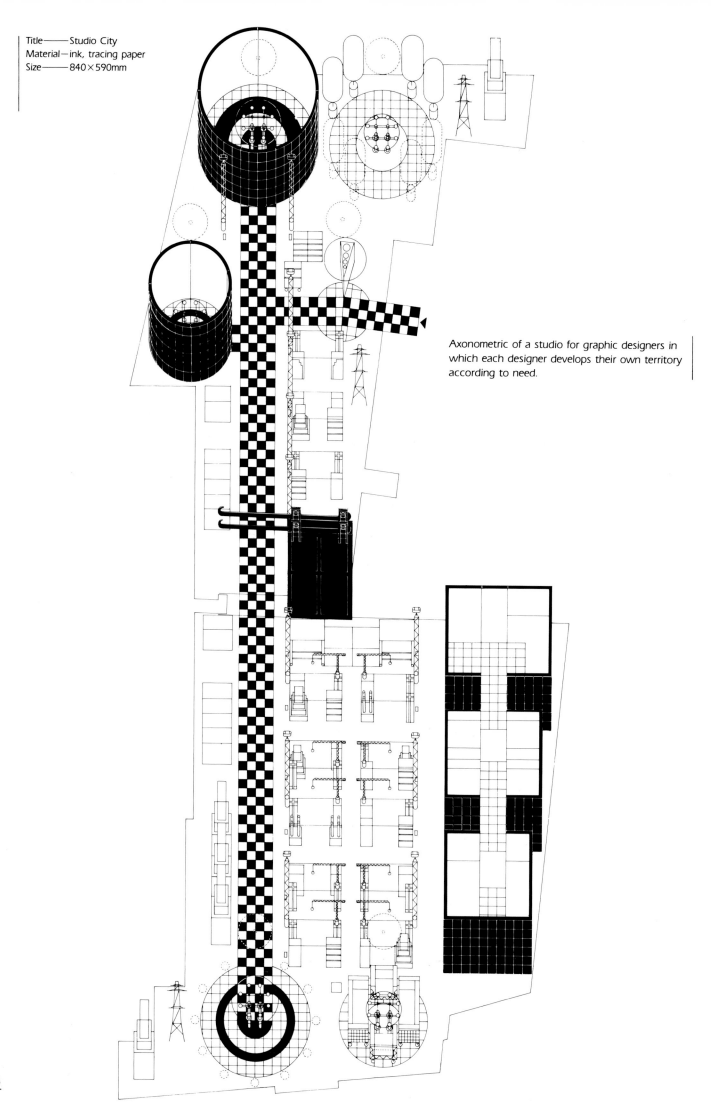

Title———Studio City
Material—ink, tracing paper
Size———840×590mm

Axonometric of a studio for graphic designers in which each designer develops their own territory according to need.

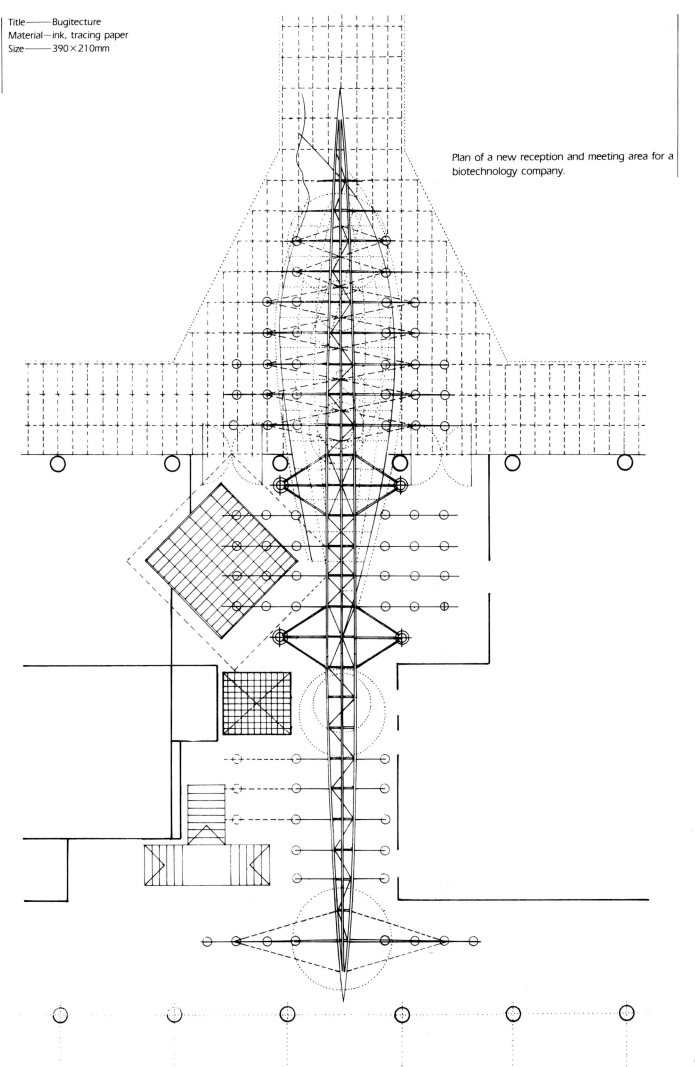

Title——Bugitecture
Material—ink, tracing paper
Size——390×210mm

Plan of a new reception and meeting area for a biotechnology company.

# Herron Associates

Title——Sets Fit for the Queen
Material—drawing paper, ink, airbrush, collage
Size——594×841mm(each)

I am fascinated by the idea of the environment in change - the twitching, flickering, variable, responsive environment. . . By mood, ambience, atmosphere, fantasy, dreams. . . sets. . . the "real" environment and the dream environment. . . public faces and private sets - private places and public sets. . . a seasonal change, a passing cloud, a new experience, the "magic" of place, a different condition. . . invention.
Anology. . . Disneyland's main street USA the remodelled Nash terraces in London — suburban England. . . etc.
The events as theatre/ the environment as sets/ space as stage/ the Queen as actor. . .

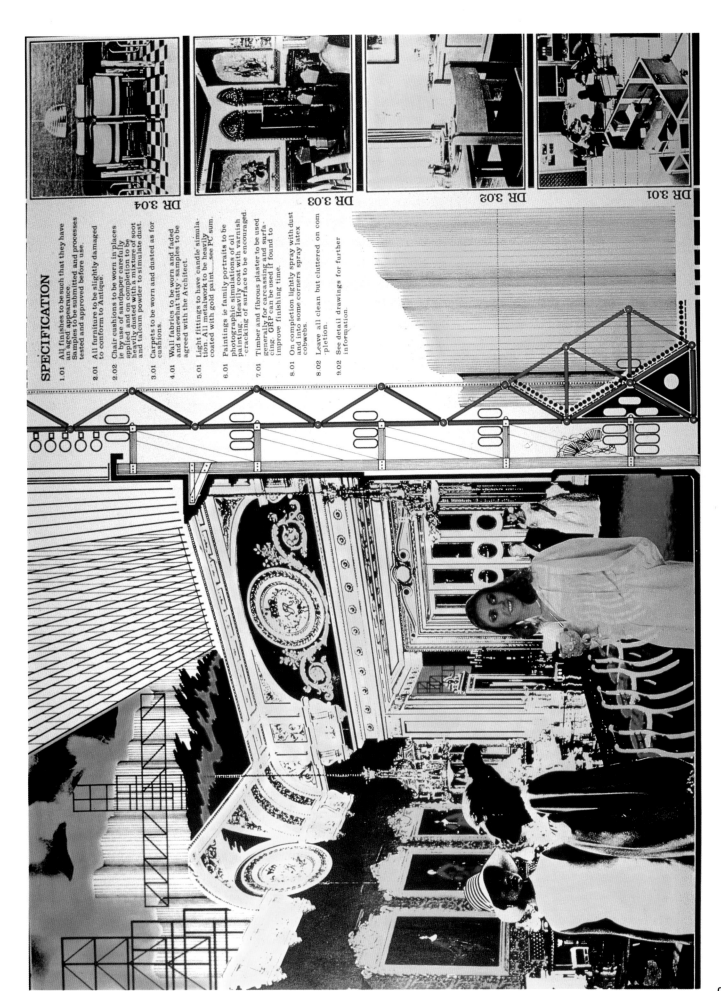

## SPECIFICATION

**1.01** All finishes to be such that they have an aged appearance. Samples to be submitted and approved before use.

**2.01** All furniture to be slightly damaged to conform to Antique.

**2.02** Chair cushions to be worn in places ie by use of sandpaper carefully applied and on completion to be heavily dusted with a mixture of soot and talcum powder to simulate dust.

**3.01** Carpets to be worn and dusted as for cushions.

**4.01** Wall fabrics to be worn and faded and somewhat tatty- samples to be agreed with the Architect.

**5.01** Light fittings to have candle simulation. All metalwork to be heavily coated with gold paint.... see PC sum.

**6.01** Paintings ie family portraits to be photographic simulations of oil painting. Heavily coat with varnish cracking of surface to be encouraged.

**7.01** Timber and fibrous plaster to be used generally for carcassing and surfacing. GRP can be used if found to improve finishing time.

**8.01** On completion lightly spray with dust and into some corners spray latex cobwebs.

**8.02** Leave all clean but cluttered on completion.

**9.02** See detail drawings for further information.

DR 304

DR 303

DR 302

DR 301

# Feilden Clegg Design

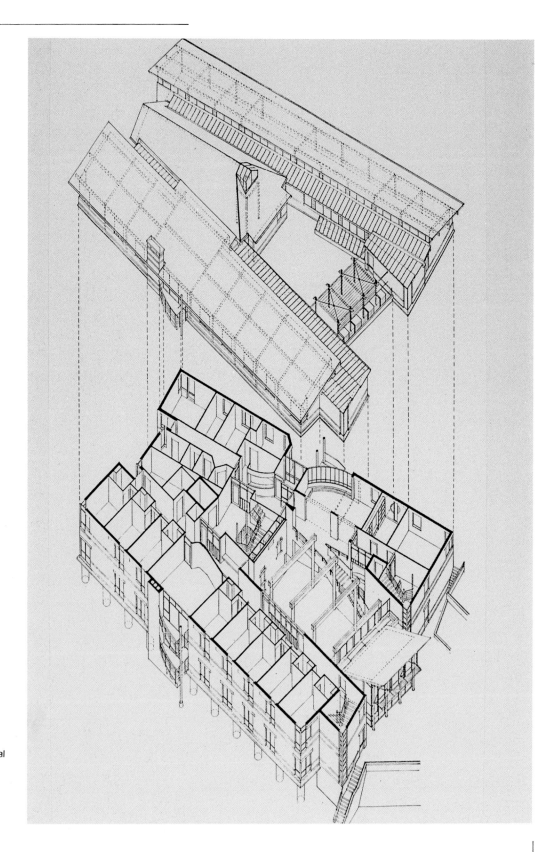

Title———Bridgecare, Residential
Home Day Centre,
Bath
Material—ink, tracing paper
Size———594×841mm

A heightened image of this riverside building is seen as a Venetian Palazzo, an English Country House or Parisian Hotel. That is, having a series of private rooms focused around public rooms, used by a community of like-minded people, functioning individually and as a large family unit. These images inspire a vision for the dignity of life, not often associated with elderly persons housing, and gives the building an appropriate architectural identity and scale.

Title———Real World Studios, Box Mill, Wiltshire
Material—card drawing, rendering
Size———594×841mm

This recording studio complex was designed in
conjunction with the clients, Peter Gabriel and Mike
Large. The studios in the old Mill building use raw
and natural materials to enhance the solid industrial
quality of the existing structure. The new building is
seen as a solid growth emerging from the back of
the Mill and opening itself out onto the Mill pond
behind. Both form and details are derived from
acoustical and technical requirements of the internal
space. The architectural delight is in contrast: new
and old, solidity and lightness, organic and rational,
water and earth.

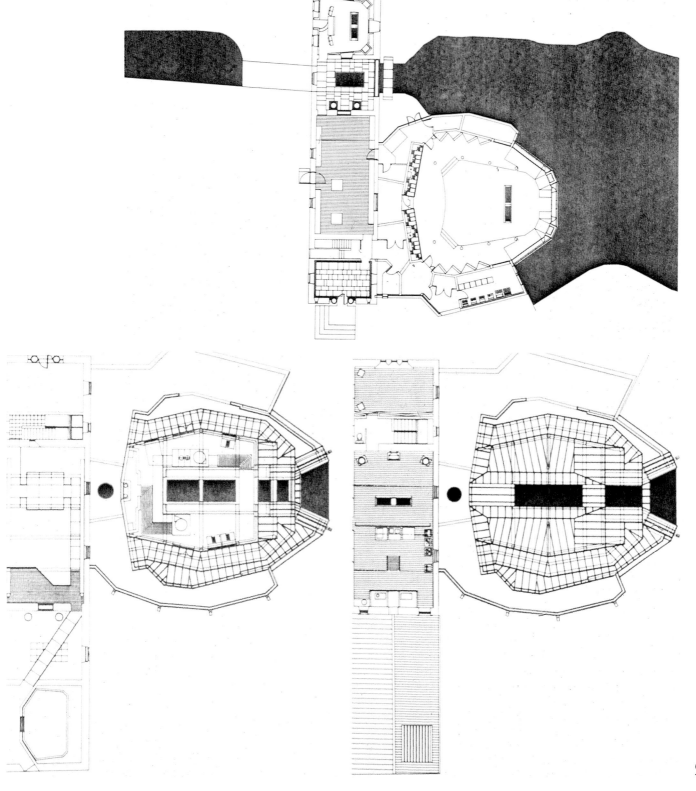

# Leon Krier

Title———House on Strangilo - Corfu Island
Material—watercolour, 300gm. card
Size———round drawing 210mm diameter

Summer house for wealthy client built as a series of
independent pavilions dedicated to one single use.
(Watercolours by Rita Wolf).

Title———House on Strangilo - Corfu Island.
Material—watercolour, 300gm. card
Size———290×310mm

# Flashman Associates

Title———The Chelsea Pavilion
Material—ink, tracing paper
Size———841×1189mm

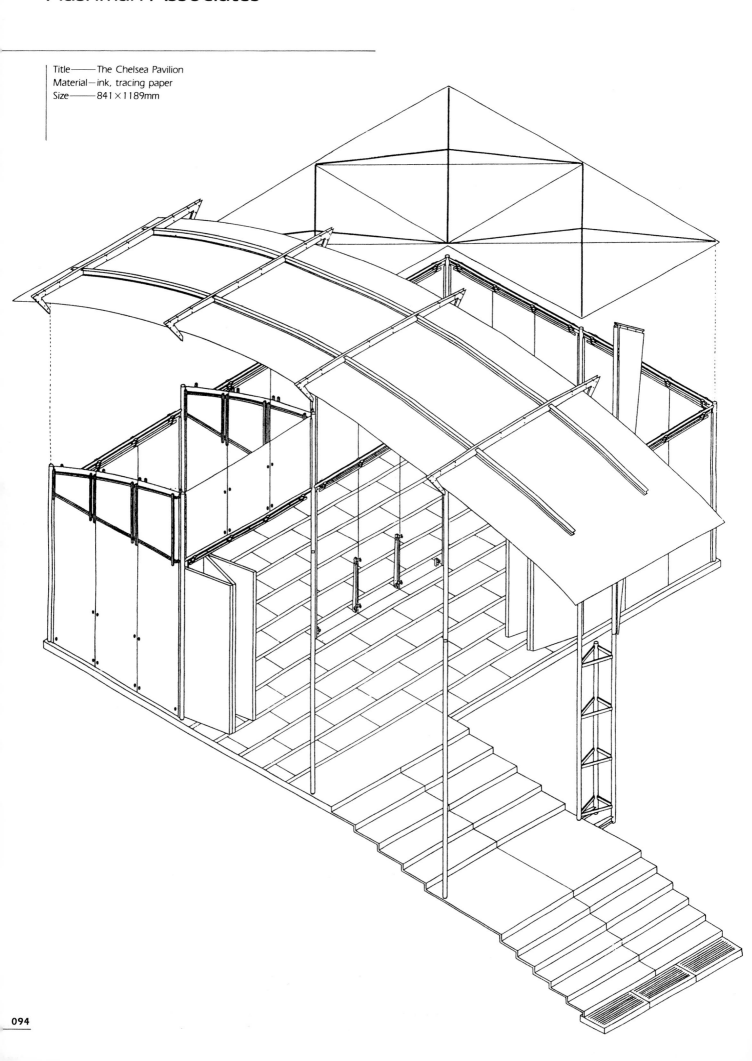

The Chelsea Pavilion is a temporary structure in the grounds of the Royal Hospital in Chelsea, London. The project was completed in a mere eleven weeks, and only three weeks of this were used for on site construction. All components were fabricated in workshops using steel, timber and glass. The footprint of the pavilion was determined by existing trees in the grounds, and by laws which prevent foundation excavations in a Royal Park.

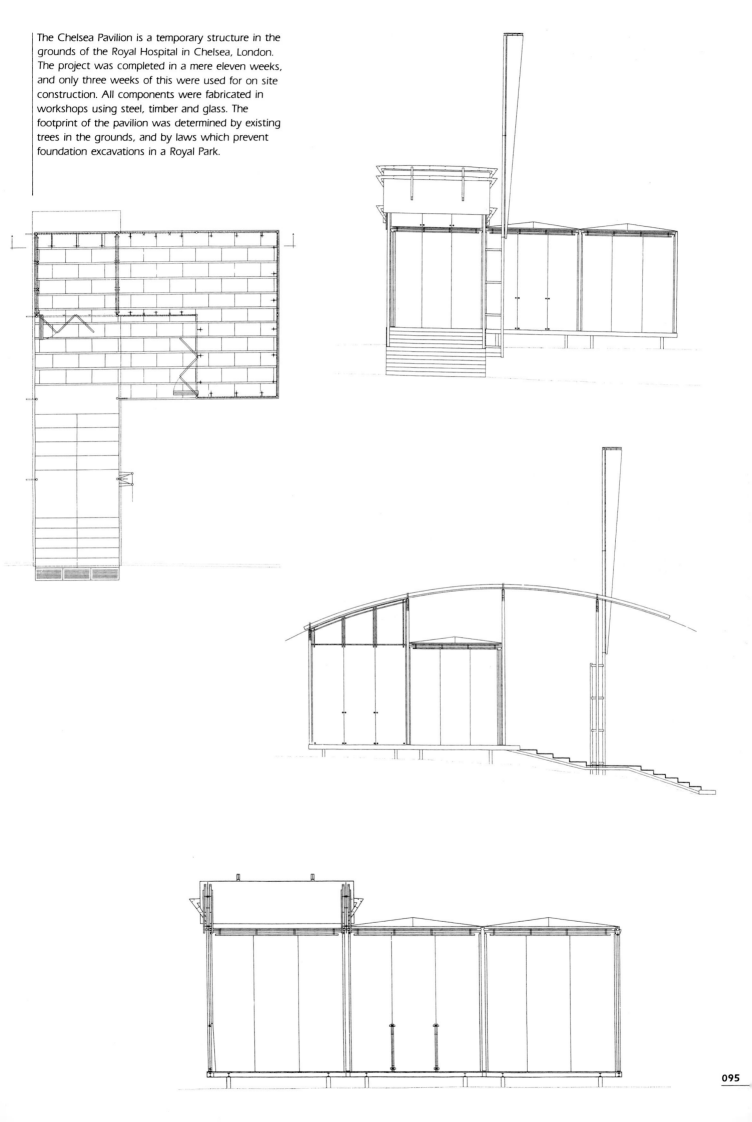

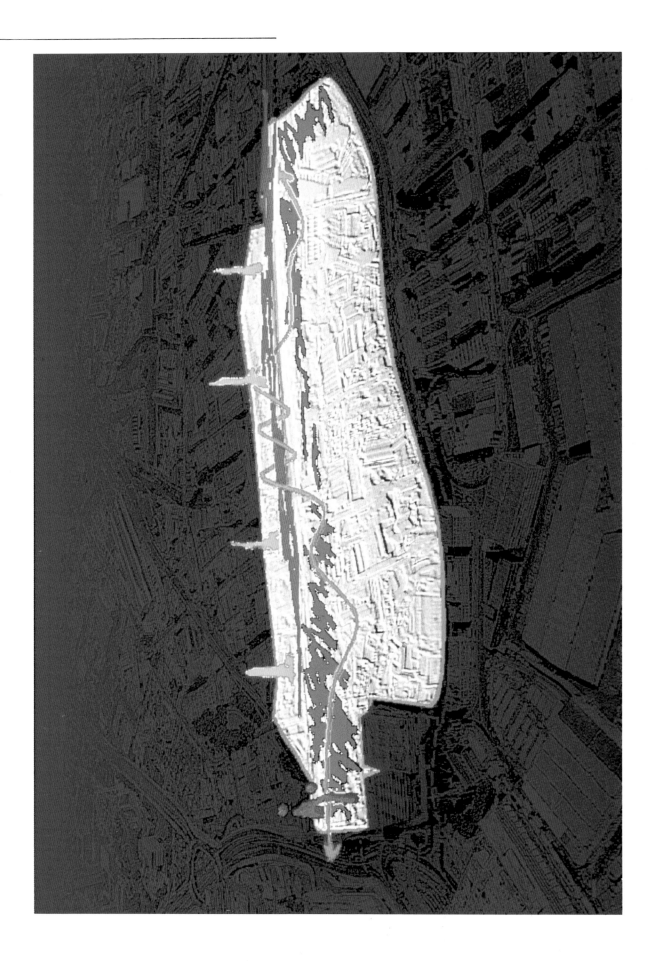

Title——Digbeth Media Area
Material—mac II cx "Pixcel Paint Pro"
Size——Variable

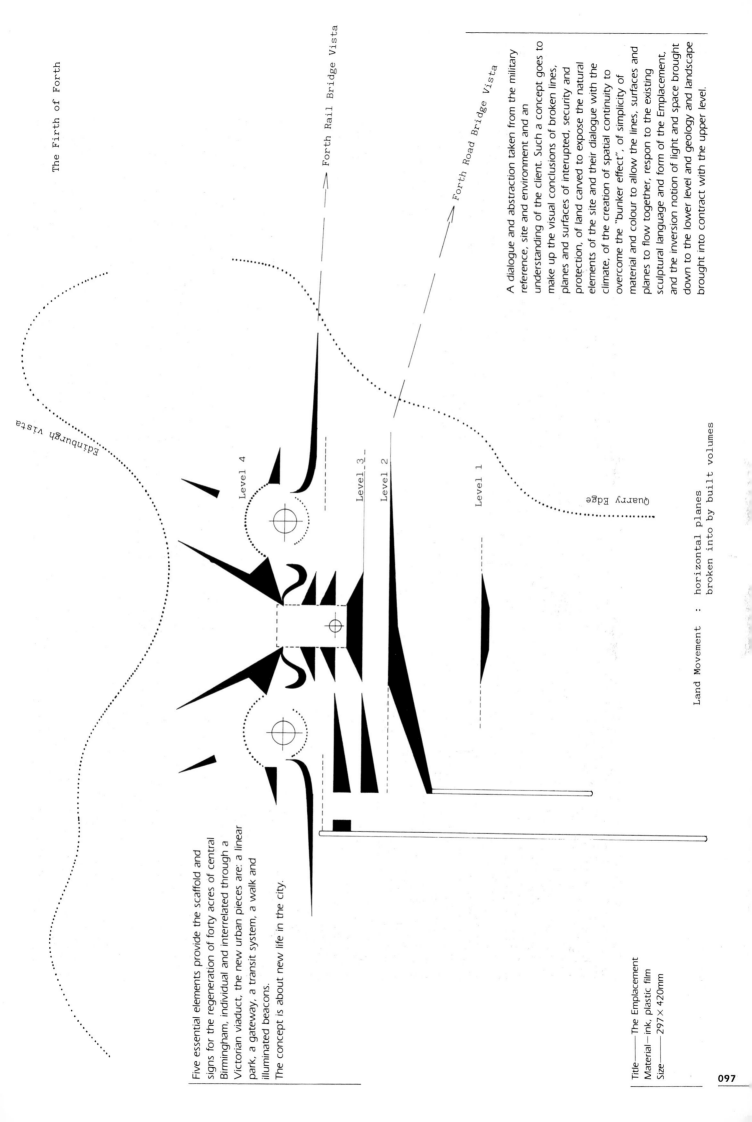

The Firth of Forth

Edinburgh Vista

Forth Rail Bridge Vista

Forth Road Bridge Vista

Level 4

Level 3

Level 2

Level 1

Quarry Edge

A dialogue and abstraction taken from the military reference, site and environment and an understanding of the client. Such a concept goes to make up the visual conclusions of broken lines, planes and surfaces of interrupted, security and protection, of land carved to expose the natural elements of the site and their dialogue with the climate, of the creation of spatial continuity to overcome the "bunker effect", of simplicity of material and colour to allow the lines, surfaces and planes to flow together, respon to the existing sculptural language and form of the Emplacement, and the inversion notion of light and space brought down to the lower level and geology and landscape brought into contract with the upper level.

Five essential elements provide the scaffold and signs for the regeneration of forty acres of central Birmingham, individual and interrelated through a Victorian viaduct, the new urban pieces are: a linear park, a gateway, a transit system, a walk and illuminated beacons.
The concept is about new life in the city.

Title —— The Emplacement
Material—ink, plastic film
Size —— 297 × 420mm

Land Movement  :  horizontal planes
                  broken into by built volumes

# Spencer Fung

Title——Caravanserai, Topkapi Palace, Istanbul
Material—ink, Carlsson paper
Size——594×1684mm

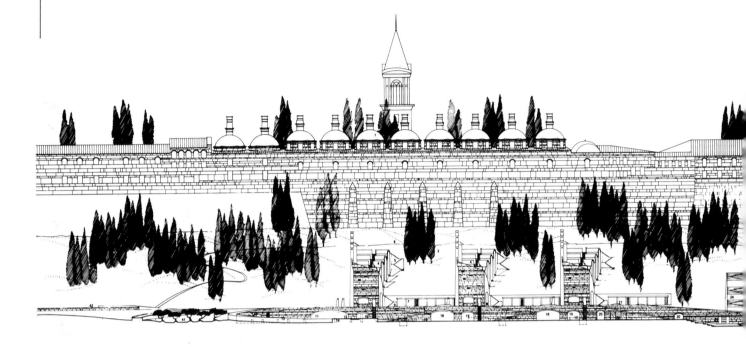

Located in the grounds of the Topkapi Palace, the Caravanserai reveals a pleasant relationship between old and new. The construction provides a haven for travellers and has become a small city with its infrastructure of drives, promenades, tavernas, communal kitchens and public bathing-houses. The heavy stone structure is also laced with fragile material to conjure up the Ottoman precedent in a modernist theme. The winner of the 1987 International RIBA Student Competition, the Caravanserai incorporates the need to cater for mass tourism without having a detrimental effect on the environment.

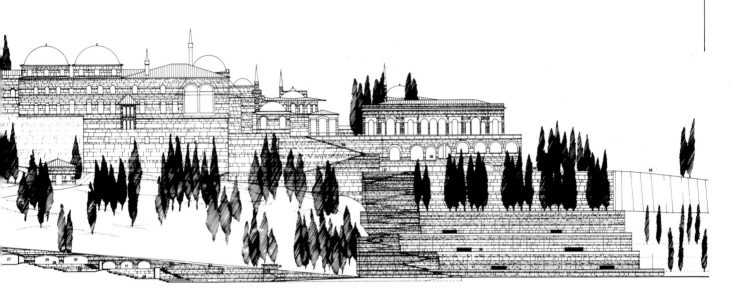

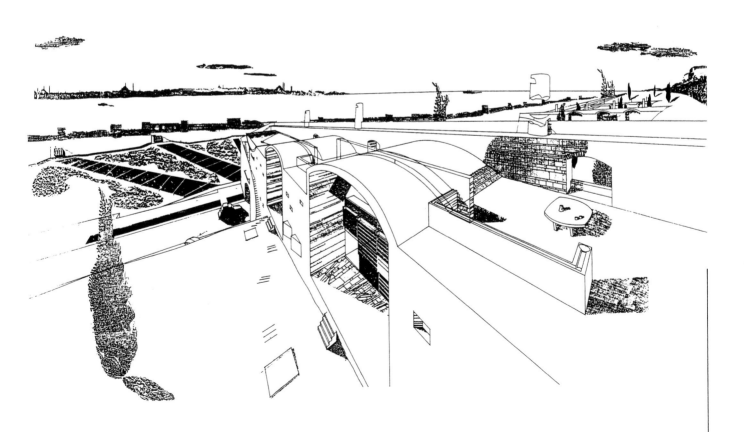

Title——Caravanserai, Topkapi Palace, Istanbul
Material—ink, Carlsson paper
Size———841×1088mm

# Florian Beigel Architects

Title——Half Moon Theatre
Material—drawing line ink, tracing paper
Size———841×1189mm
Drawing—Hendric Welp

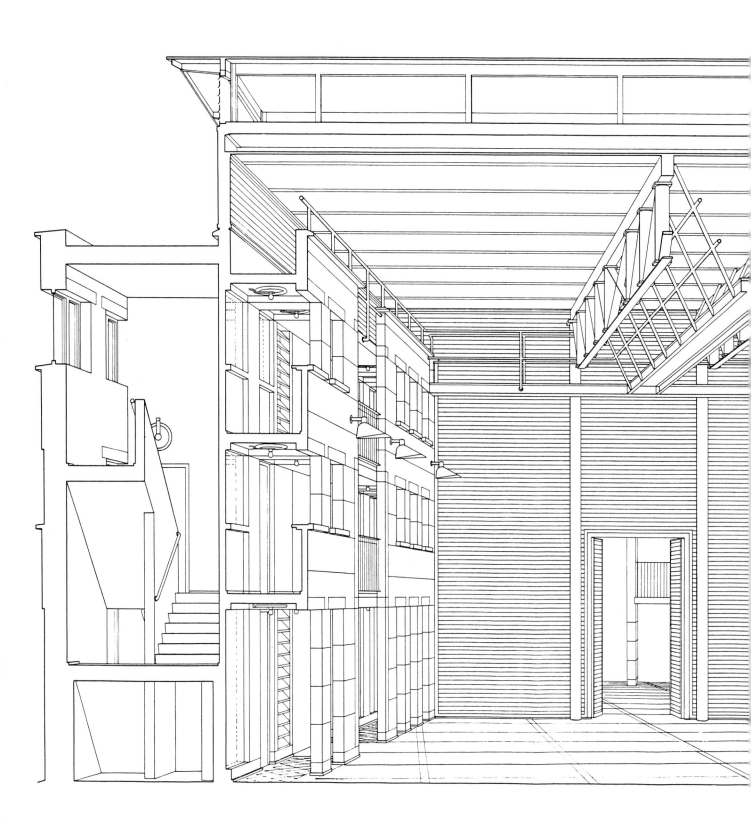

The ink lines depict the disposition of the
architectural elements in outline. This enables the
information available to be registered by one's
intellect. The sections and perspectives clarify the
elements which summon up the aura of a regular
street with houses facing each other. The theatre
becomes a courtyard with a roof.

# Ada Gansach-Wilson

Title——A Crematorium for Existentialists
Material—ink, tracing paper
Size——594×841mm(all)

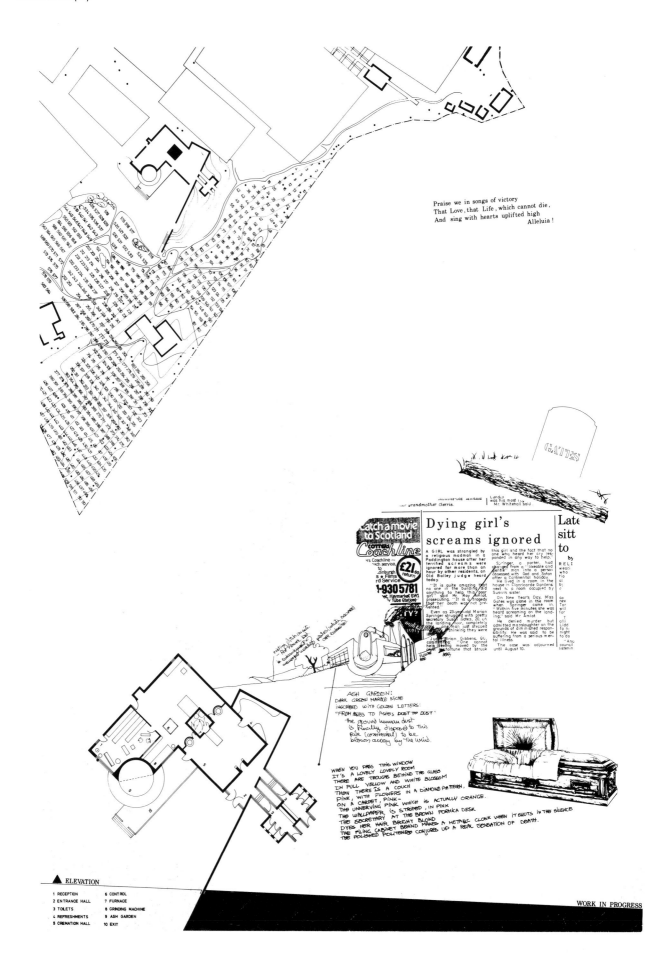

Praise we in songs of victory
That Love, that Life, which cannot die,
And sing with hearts uplifted high
Alleluia !

ASH GARDEN:
DARK GREEN MARBLE NICHE
INSCRIBED WITH GOLDEN LETTERS:
"FROM ASHES TO ASHES DUST TO DUST"
the ground human dust
is finally disposed to this
Rite (communal) to be
blown away by the wind.

WHEN YOU PASS THIS WINDOW
IT'S A LOVELY LOVELY ROOM
THERE ARE TROUGHS BEHIND THE GLASS
IN FULL YELLOW AND WHITE BLOSSOM
THEN THERE IS A COUCH
PINK, WITH FLOWERS IN A DIAMOND PATTERN,
ON A CARPET, PINK —
THE UNNERVING PINK WHICH IS ACTUALLY ORANGE
THE WALLPAPER IS STRIPED, IN PINK
THE SECRETARY AT THE BROWN FORMICA DESK
DYES HER HAIR BRIGHT BLOND
THE FILING CABINET BEHIND MAKES A METALLIC CLONK WHEN IT SHUTS IN THE SILENCE
THE POLISHED POLITENESS CONJURES UP A REAL SENSATION OF DEATH.

▲ ELEVATION

| | |
|---|---|
| 1 RECEPTION | 6 CONTROL |
| 2 ENTRANCE HALL | 7 FURNACE |
| 3 TOILETS | 8 GRINDING MACHINE |
| 4 REFRESHMENTS | 9 ASH GARDEN |
| 5 CREMATION HALL | 10 EXIT |

WORK IN PROGRESS

Title———Housing the Middle Classes(Singles)
Material—ink, tracing paper
Size———594×841mm(all)

A critical look at architecture is needed; we should no longer indulge in formalistic Utopia. Exposure of absurd and delightful prejudices is called for. The recycled and juxtaposed norms of building types become subverted and naive; kitsch and cliches are crucial for accessible communication. I try to draw essays in "Critical Architecture". . . This architecture is not for sale.

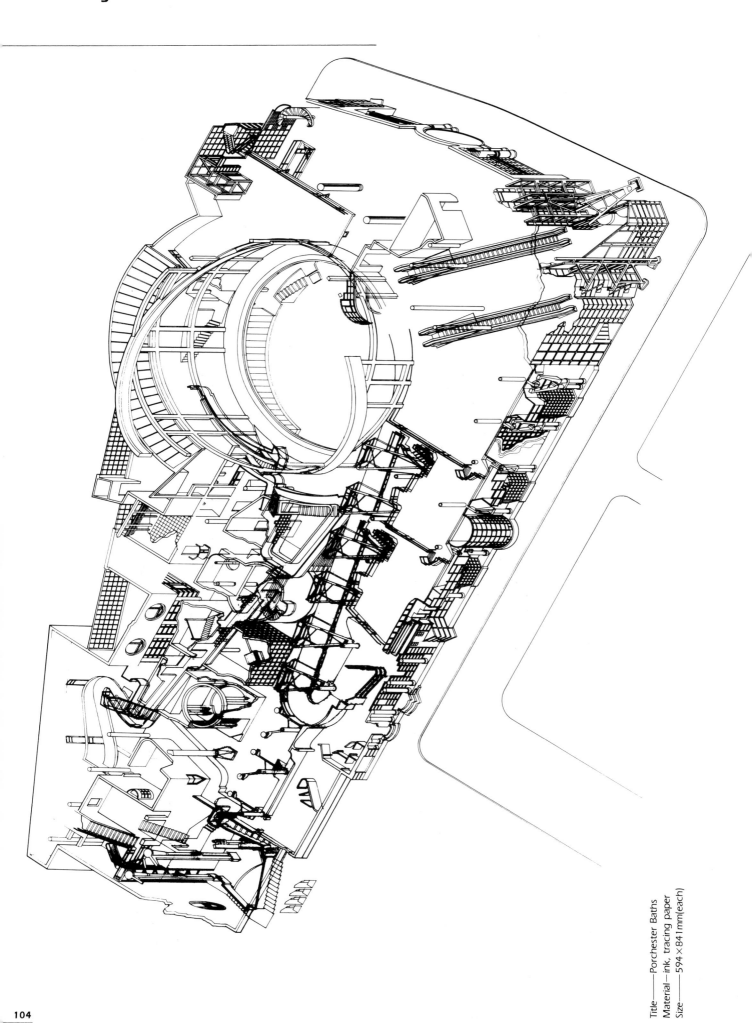

Title ———— Porchester Baths
Material — ink, tracing paper
Size ———— 594 × 841mm(each)

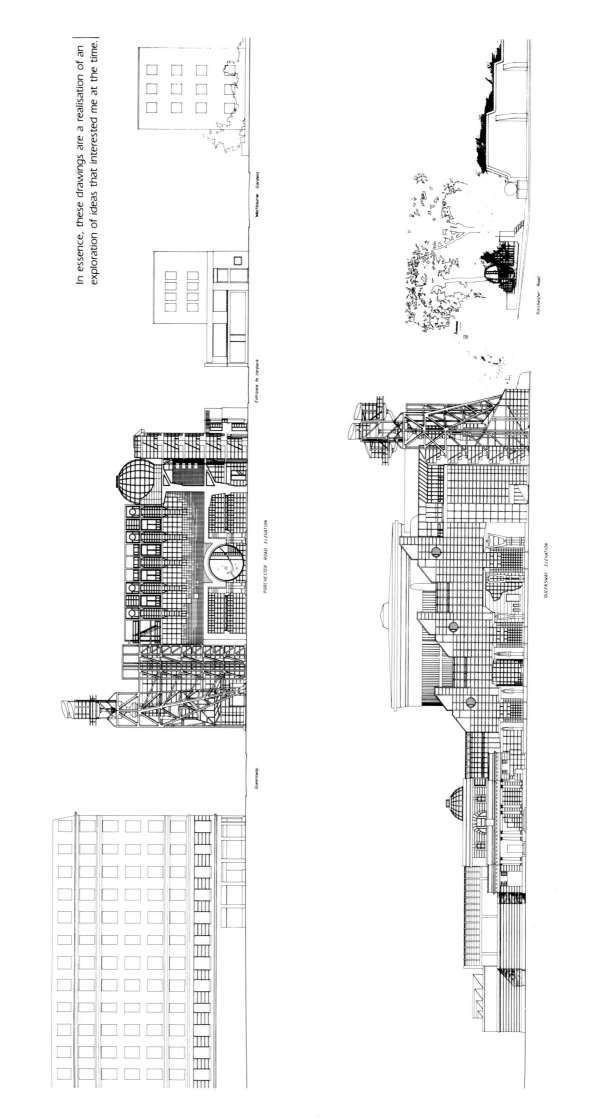

In essence, these drawings are a realisation of an exploration of ideas that interested me at the time.

Westbourne Gardens

Entrance to carpark

Queensway

PORCHESTER ROAD ELEVATION

Porchester Road

QUEENSWAY ELEVATION

105

# Justina Karakiewicz

Title——Tower of Babel
Material—pen, ink
Size——1189×841mm

Creativity is somewhat mysterious, a gift reserved for gods. Wanting to possess it is part of man's challenge, part of the Babel's Tower of pride which rises from the floor to reach the sky.

# Munkenbeck+Marshall Architects

Title———Cooperage, London
Material—ink, tracing paper
Size———420×285mm

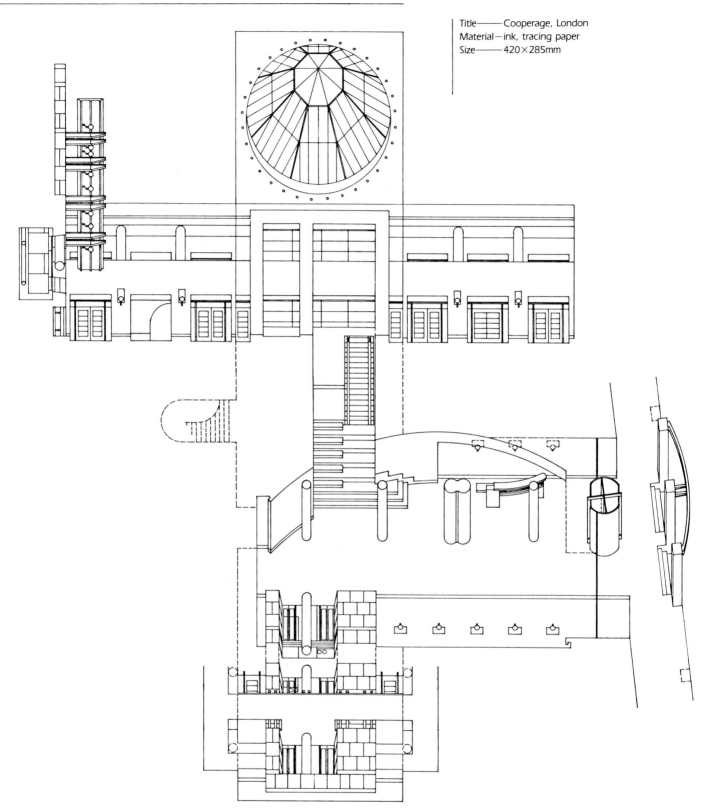

The design involves the conversion of an existing Thameside warehouse into offices with riverside apartments above. An atrium is formed at first floor level allowing daylight to the office space. Access to the office space is at street level and is via a curved lobby from which stairs leads up to a courtyard within the atrium. The space is detailed using external materials as if it were an external court. Floors are stone, and walls are plastered with crushed granite. This breaks down the mass of the existing building and provides a focus for the entire building.

Title———Cooperage, London
Material—ink, tracing paper
Size———420×285mm

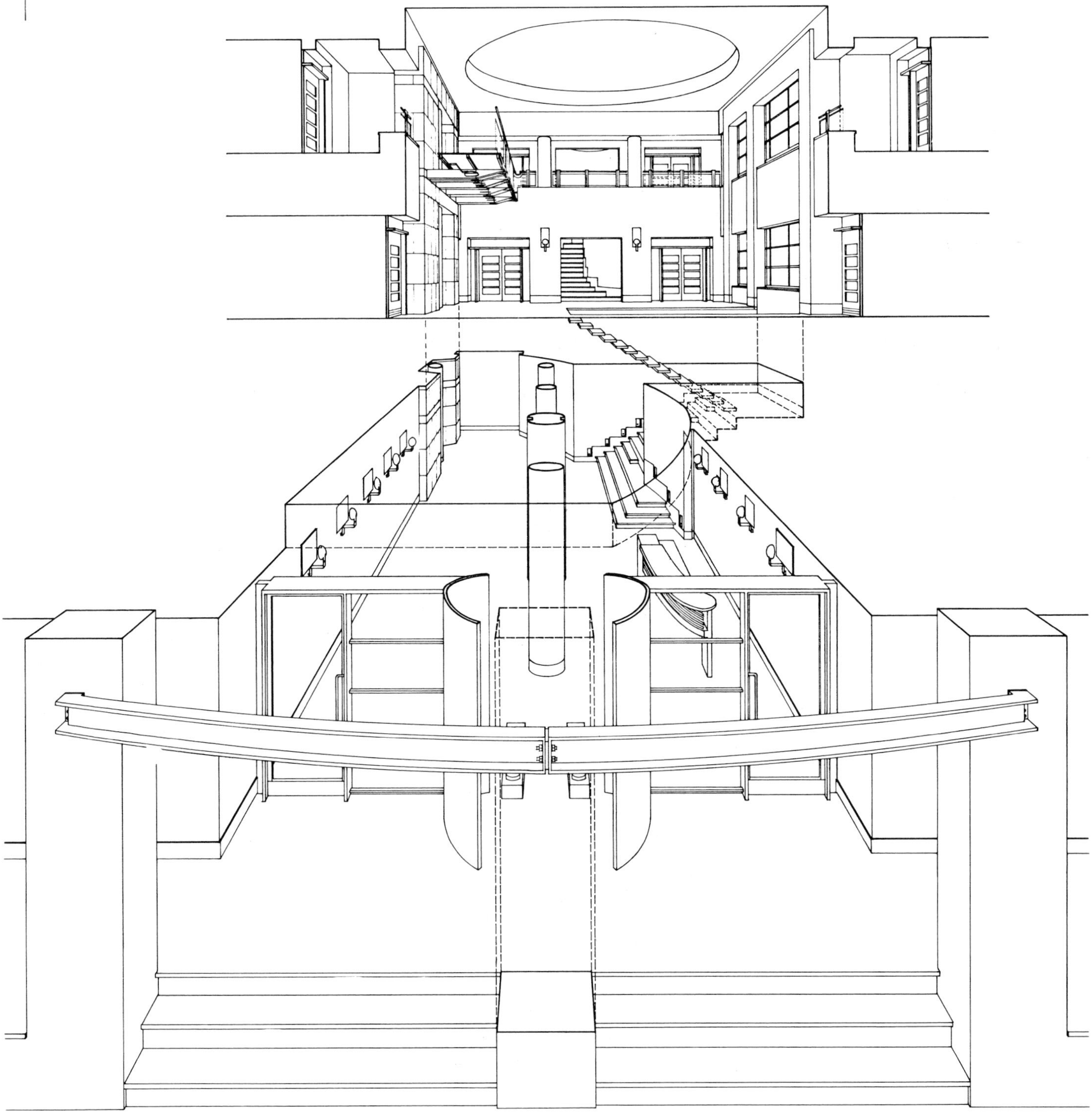

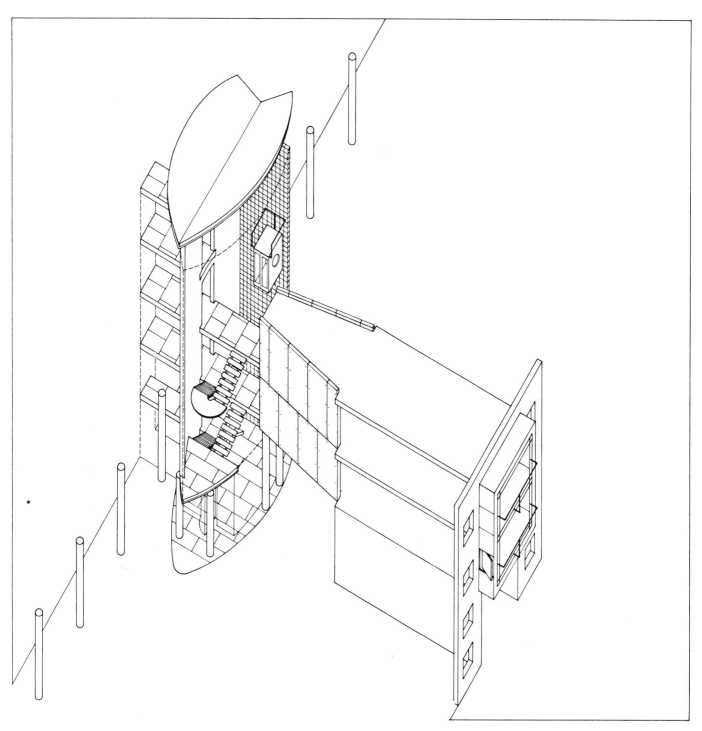

Title———Jessica Square, London, Lift Stair Link
Material—ink, tracing paper
Size———420×285mm

The project consists of two office buildings linked by
a central tower containing stairs, lift and services.
The site is situated behind an existing street of two
and three storey buildings and this defines the
height of the lower of the two blocks. Towards the
centre of the site the taller block looks out over the
lower building giving views into the town to the
north and open parkland to the south. A mews is
formed with bamboo gardens giving daylight and
fresh air to the interior of the offices. The top of the
service tower has a wing formed in steel. The wing
can be seen from the River Thames to the north and
will be seen floating above Wandsworth when
viewed from the common to the east. The
supersonic church spire.

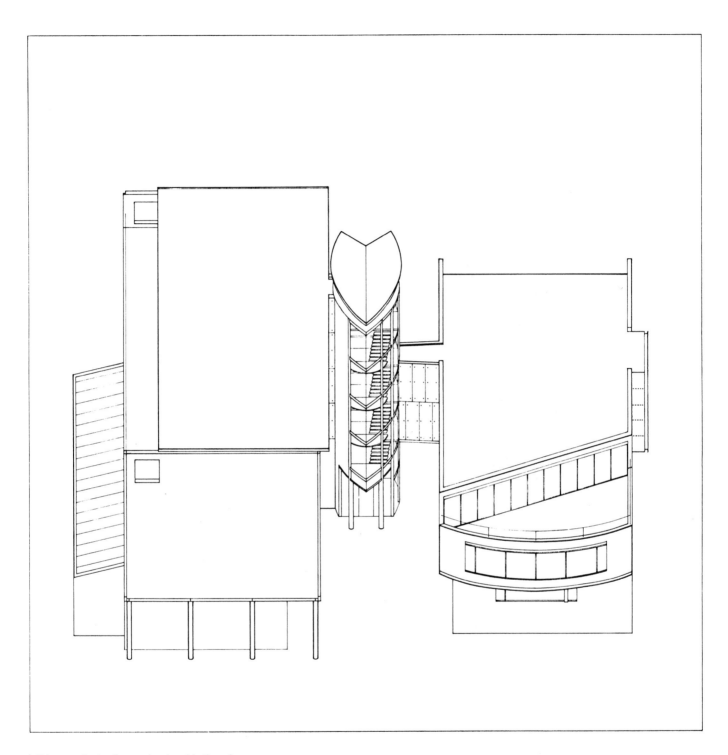

Title——Jessica Square, London, North and
          South Buildings with Lift Stair Link Between
Material—ink, tracing paper
Size——420×285mm

# Neave Brown David Porter
# Architects

Title———Mozzo One
Material—ink, tracing paper
Size———1200×840mm

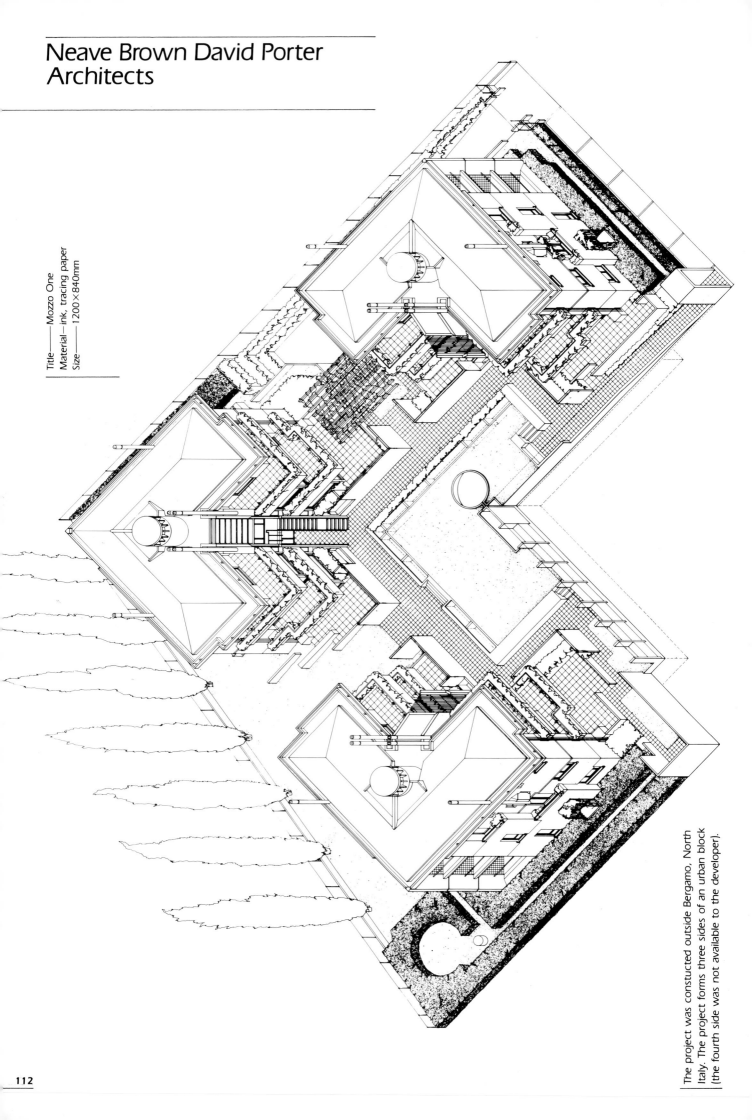

The project was constucted outside Bergamo, North Italy. The project forms three sides of an urban block (the fourth side was not available to the developer).

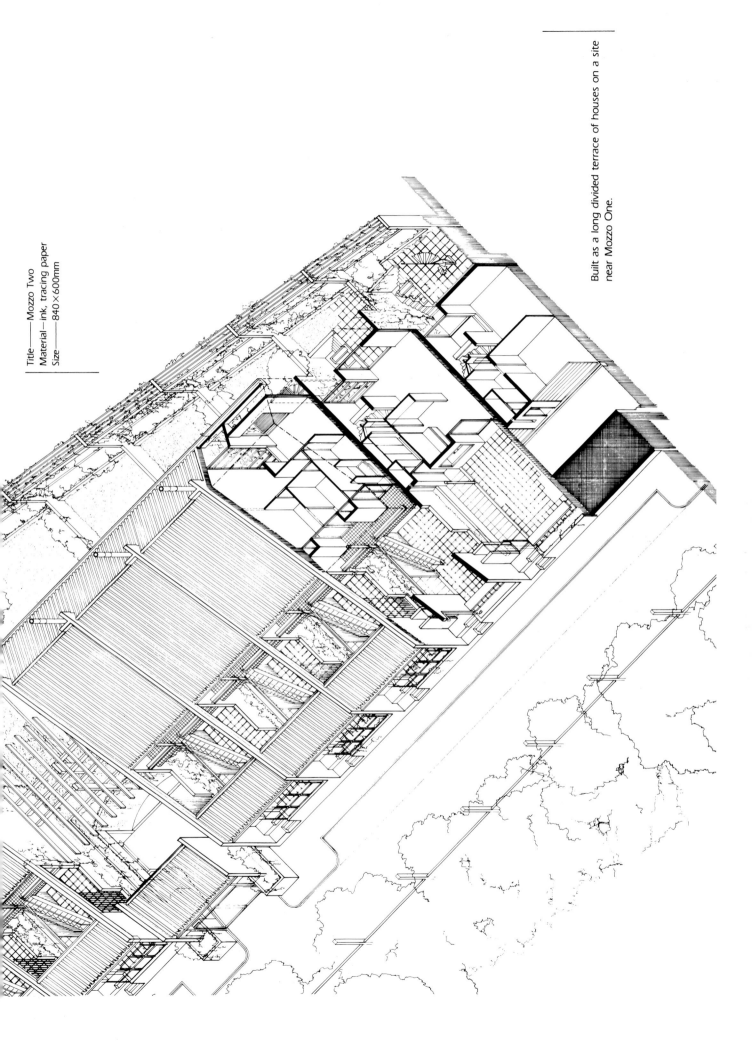

Title——Mozzo Two
Material——ink, tracing paper
Size——840×600mm

Built as a long divided terrace of houses on a site near Mozzo One.

113

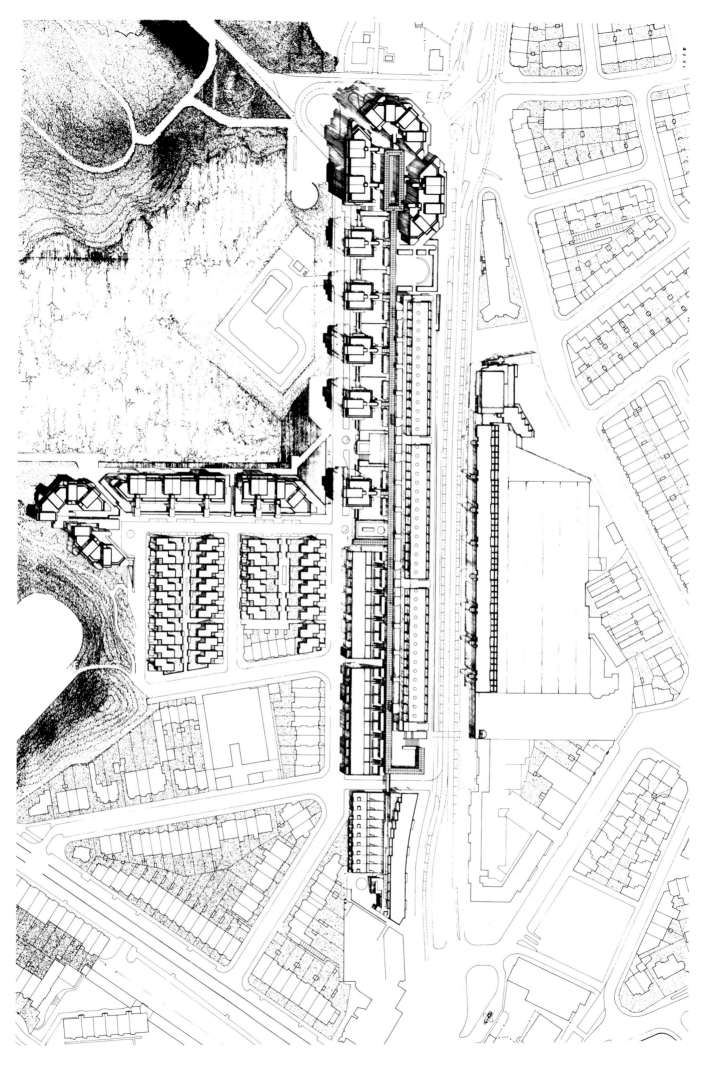

Title———Project Zwolsestraat, The Hague, Netherlands
Material—ink, tracing paper
Size———1200×840mm

The project comprises five hundred housing units, an underground car-park and a dune landscape and lake. The project occurs where the edge of the capital city meets the sand dunes that form the natural boundary between the country and the sea. The scheme provides accomodation at very high density while making a new urban edge.

Title———Student Hostel for the Hotel School of
           The Hague
Material—ink, tracing paper
Size———1200×600mm

The building is adjacent to the Zwolsestraat Housing project. It similarly forms a new edge to an urban block. The new building is constructed on the roof of an existing tram station. Work started on site in February 1990.
The scheme includes a large social hall at the entry end, a mixture of single and double rooms with their own communal room, and has to cope with the difficulty of entry up to an "artifical" level for circulation.

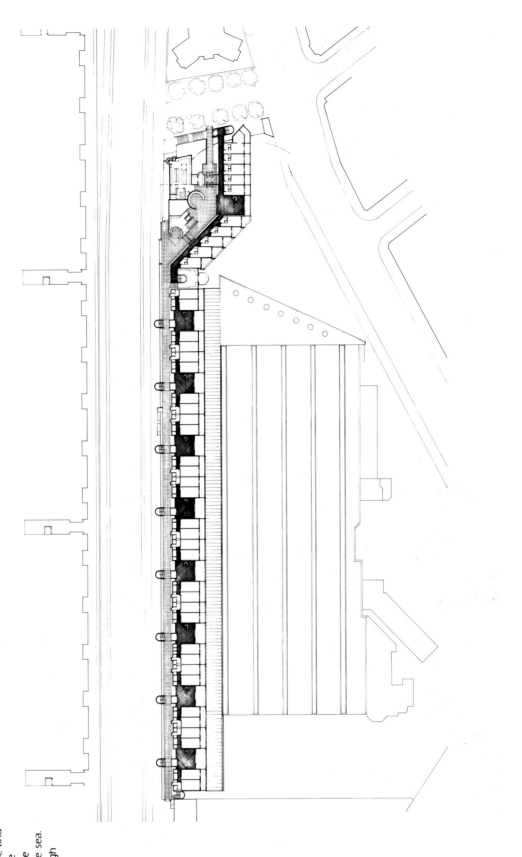

# Nicholas Grimshaw & Partners Ltd.

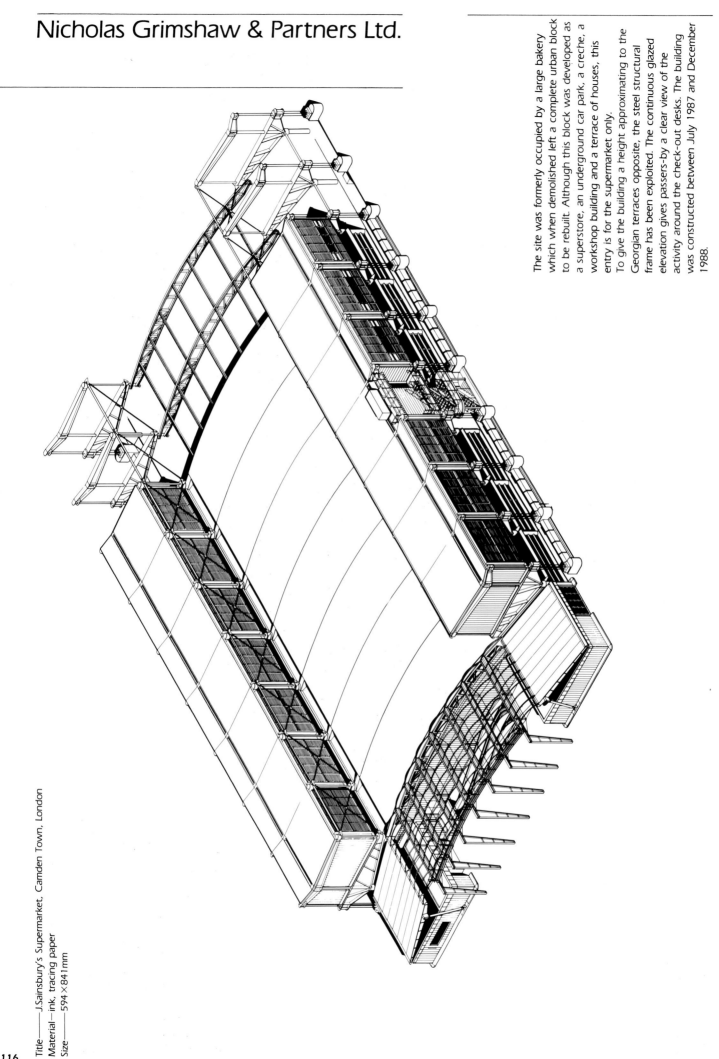

The site was formerly occupied by a large bakery which when demolished left a complete urban block to be rebuilt. Although this block was developed as a superstore, an underground car park, a creche, a workshop building and a terrace of houses, this entry is for the supermarket only.

To give the building a height approximating to the Georgian terraces opposite, the steel structural frame has been exploited. The continuous glazed elevation gives passers-by a clear view of the activity around the check-out desks. The building was constructed between July 1987 and December 1988.

Title———J.Sainsbury's Supermarket, Camden Town, London
Material—ink, tracing paper
Size———594×841mm

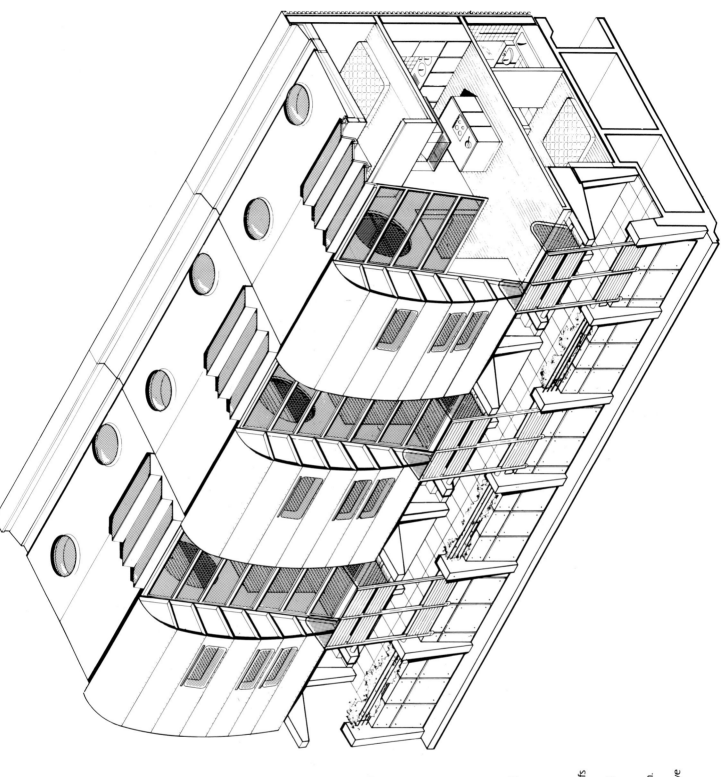

Title———The houses at the J.Sainsbury's,
    Camden Town, London

Material—ink, tracing paper

Size———594×841mm

A ten metre wide strip of land parallel to the canal was utilised to construct these residential units. They comprise ten one three bedroom houses, a one bedroom maisonette and a bedsit flat. The houses are built from dense concrete blockwork with precast concrete floors and felt covered timber roofs pitched at 10°. Solid cladding facing the canal is constructed from three millimeter thick overlapping PVF2 coated aluminium panels arranged on the "rainscreen" principle with a well ventilated cavity between the panels and the internal wall insulation. Internal finishes mainly consist of white painted plastered walls and ceilings with tongue and groove beech flooring.

# Rick Mather Architects

Title———Waddington Art Gallery, London W1
Material—ink, film
Size———594×841mm

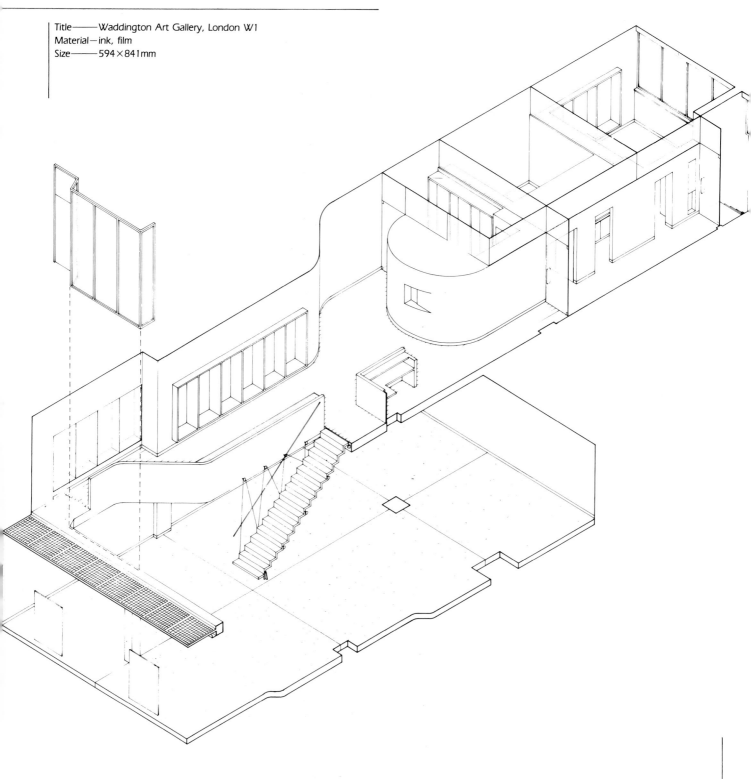

Our initial design considerations are usually a balance of three things: what is appropriate to the surroundings, what will secure the most generous spaces inside, and what is the general type that satisfies the brief most effectively.

To achieve the above considerations, our aims are to reinforce and develop the city by maintaining its density, to make the most of natural light and sunshine, and to achieve a construction in which only the essential minimum is apparent. We believe that any serious architect has an interest in and knowledge of the present and the past. We therefore use as references the works of Le Corbusier, Unwin and Rasmussen, Frank Lloyd Wright and Colin Rowe.

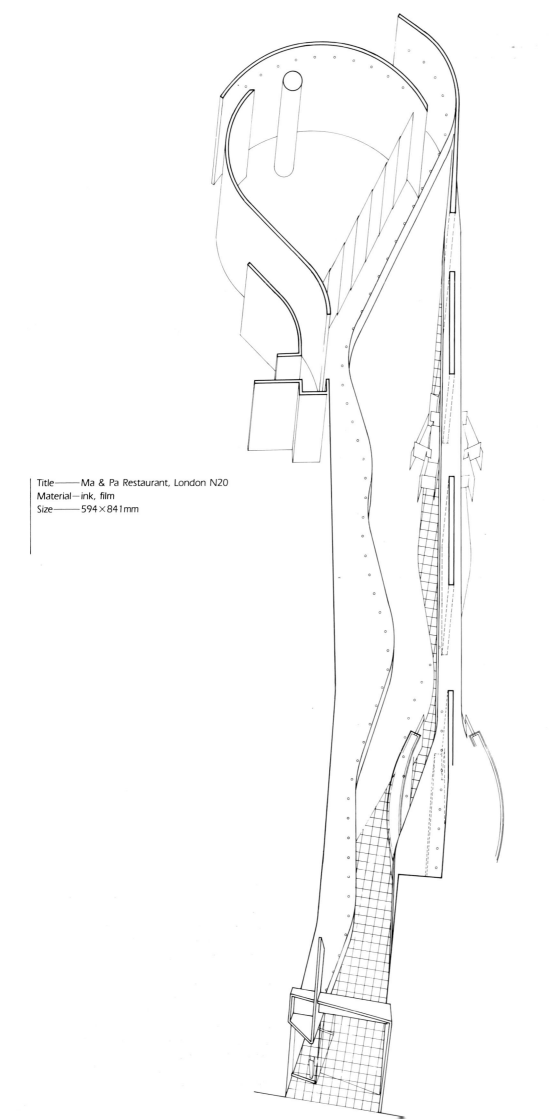

Title———Ma & Pa Restaurant, London N20
Material—ink, film
Size———594×841mm

Title———Building Massing and Elevational Study
Material—ink, film
Size———420×594mm

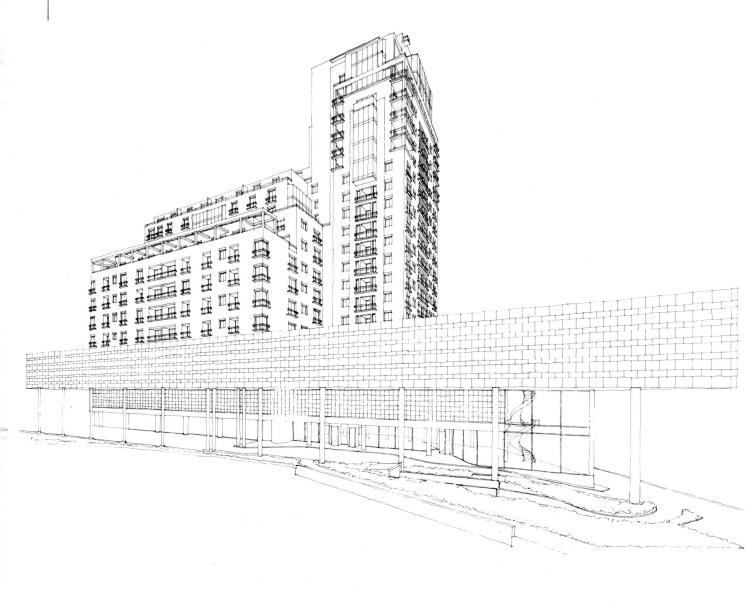

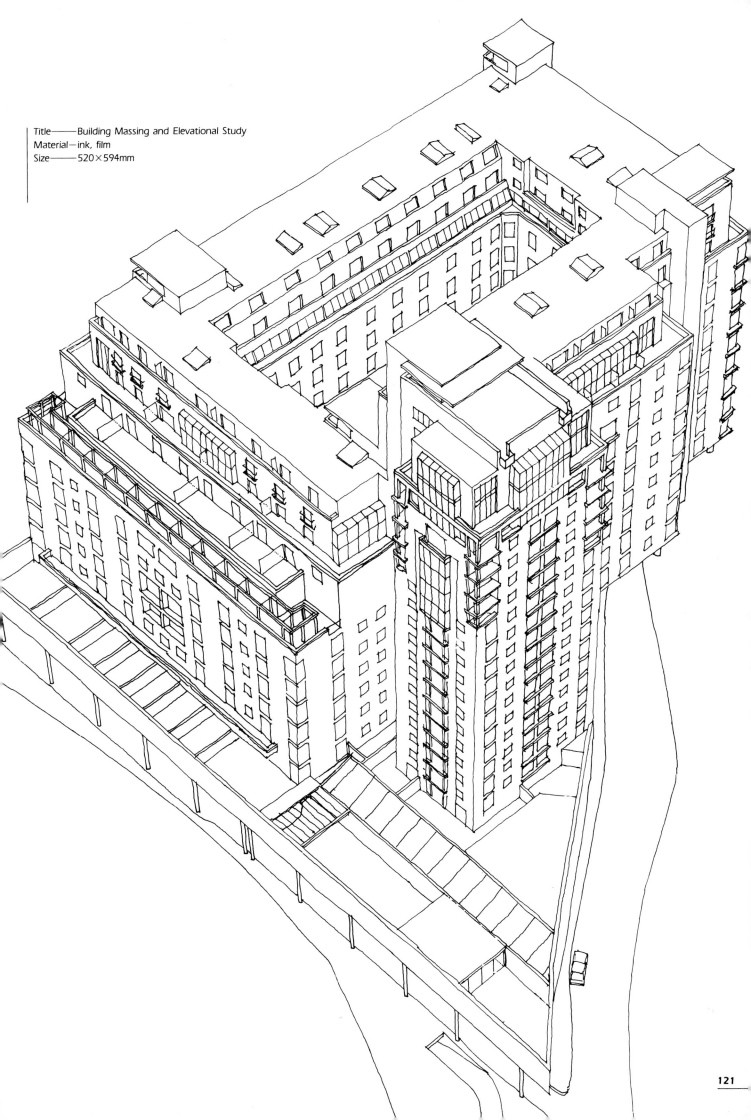

Title———Building Massing and Elevational Study
Material—ink, film
Size———520×594mm

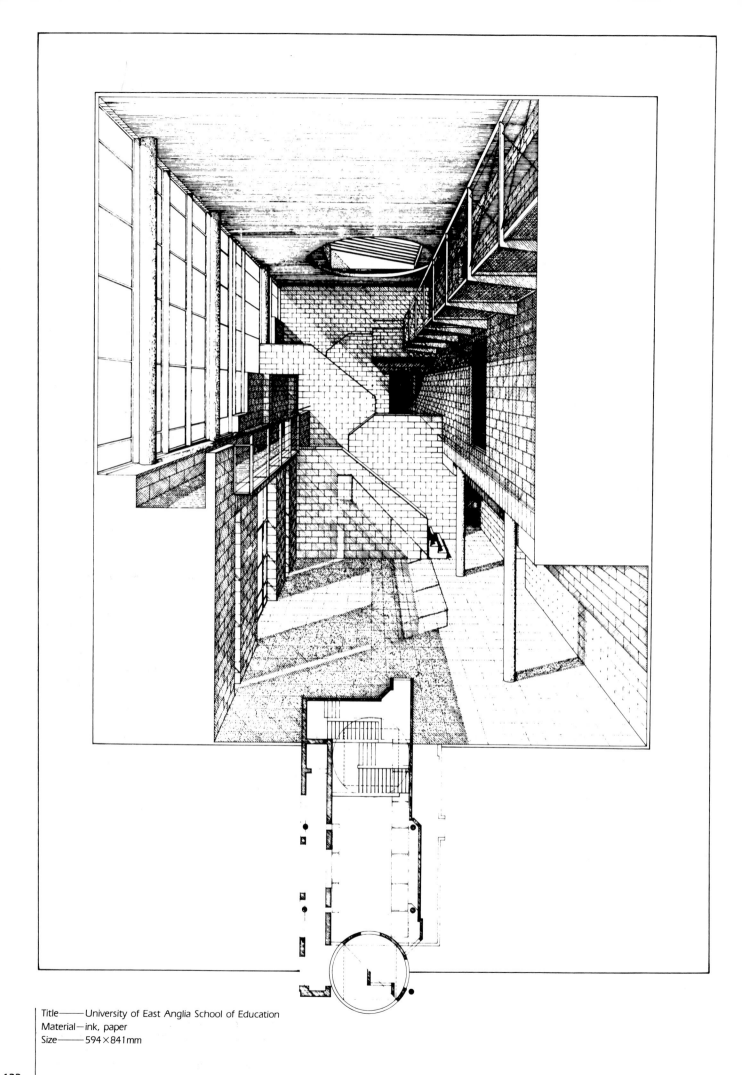

Title——University of East Anglia School of Education
Material—ink, paper
Size——594×841mm

# Stanton Williams

Title——St. Ives Gallery, Cornwall, England,
           Spatial analysis.
Material—ink pen, tracing paper
Size——475×500mm

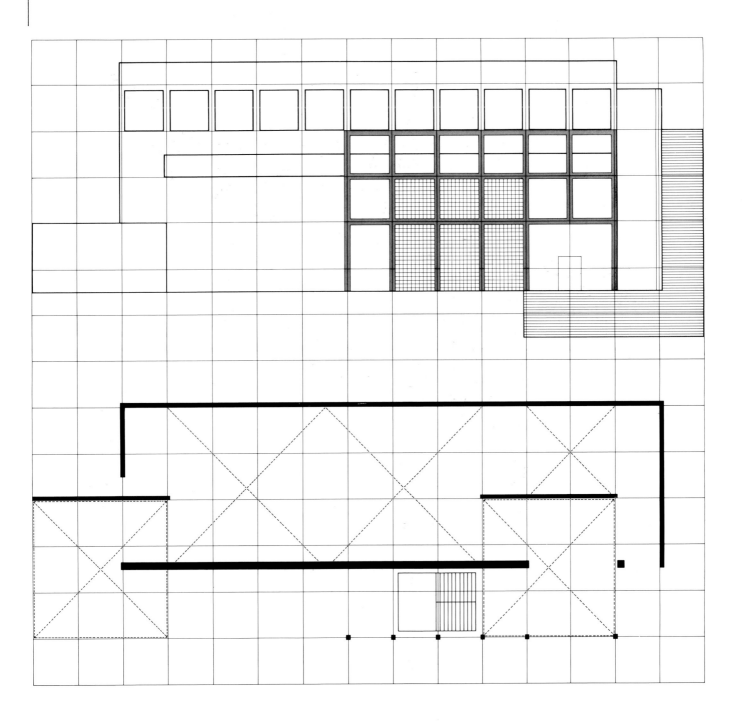

This submission was made for a closed competition organised by the Tate Gallery in London. The new gallery was proposed to accommodate their collection of paintings and sculptures by the artists in the St. Ives area.

Title———Royal Institute of British Architects,
         Library Entrance
Material—ink pen, tracing paper(each)
Size———480×370mm

Title———Royal Institute of British Architects, Gallery Space
Material—ink pen, tracing paper(each)
Size———485×425mm

The refurbishment of and new extensions to the
British Architectural Library; the Drawings Collection
and a new Exhibition Gallery.

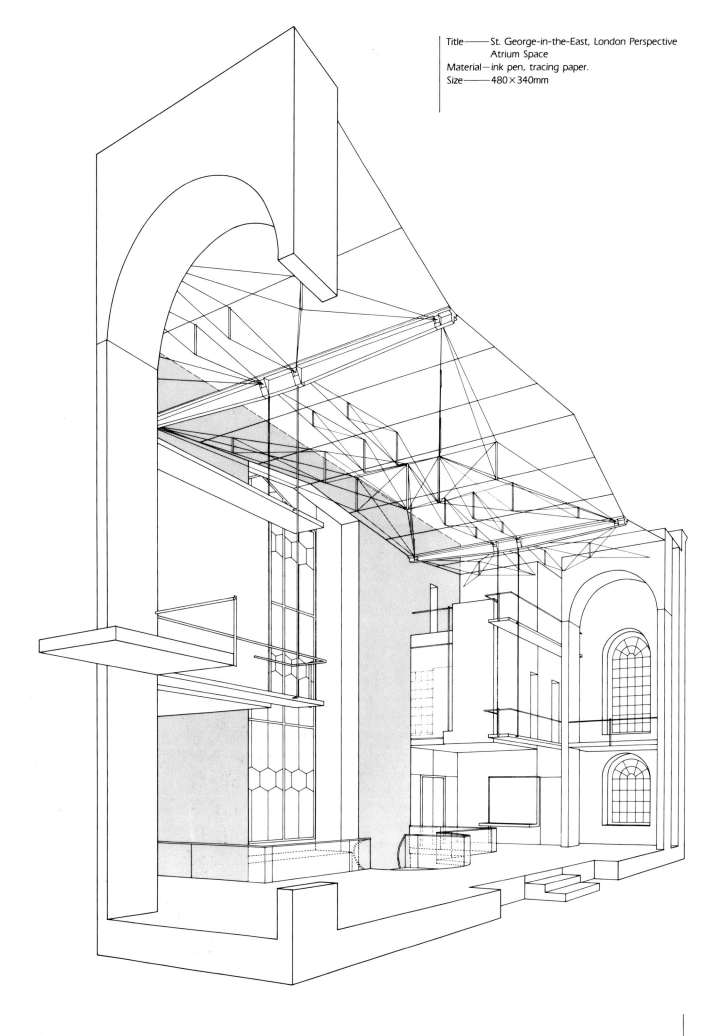

Title———St. George-in-the-East, London Perspective
　　　　　Atrium Space
Material—ink pen, tracing paper.
Size———480×340mm

A masterplan for the development of Nicholas
Hawksmoor's church and its site. This includes the
integration of a performance centre and recording
studios for the Guildhall Ensemble.

# Stirling Wilford and Associates

Title————Compton Verney
Material—ink, tracing paper(each)
Size————420×595mm(each)

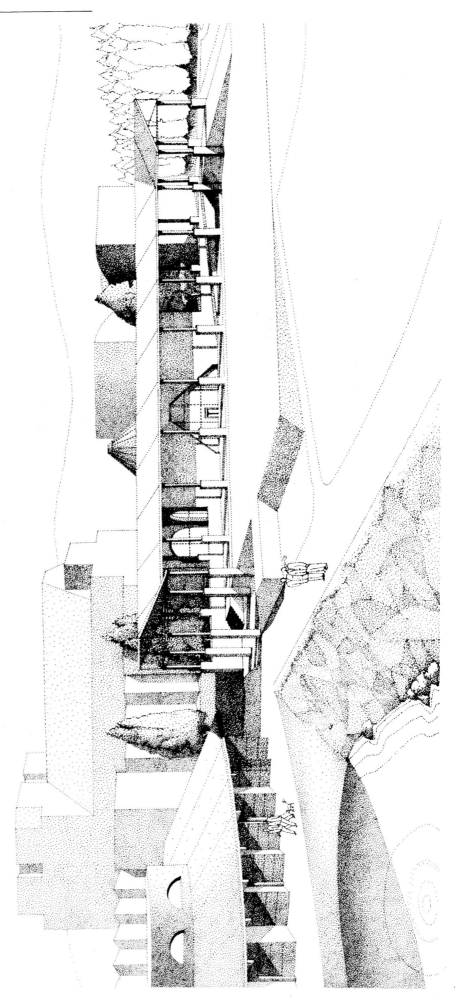

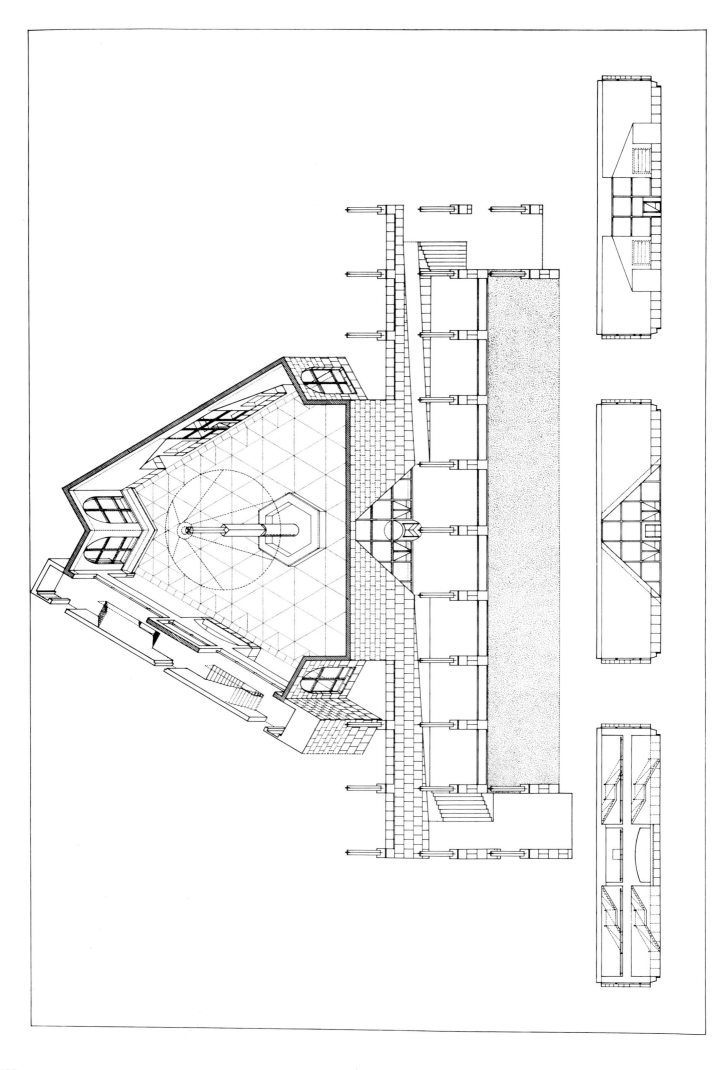

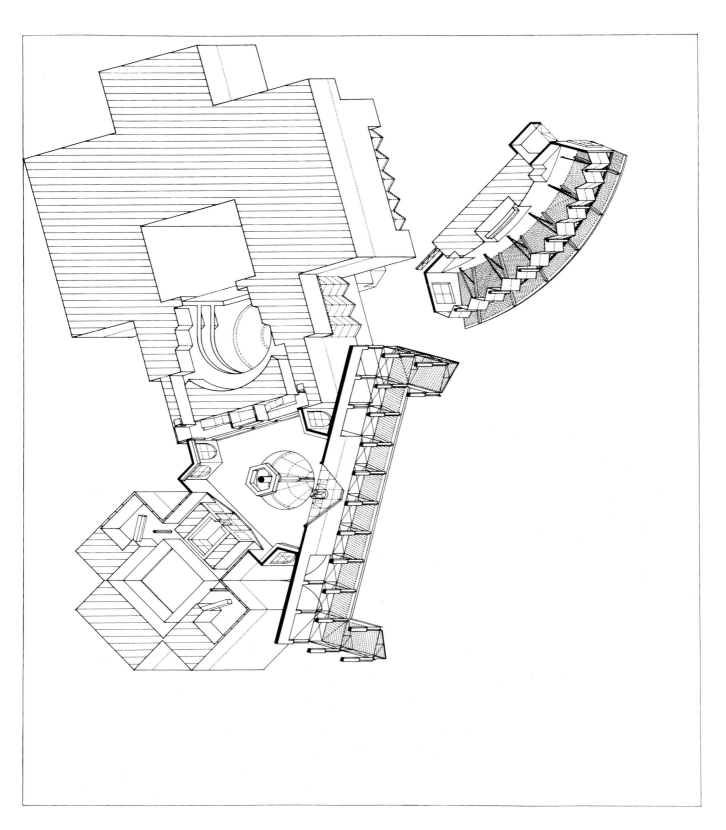

Soil investigations show limestone just below the surface, which would have made proposals to sink the building into the ground both difficult and expensive. Consequently, the apparent height of the stagehouse was reduced by the forward positioning of the loggia, the administration pavilion and the restaurant bridge. The loggia allows visitors to approach from all directions and forms a backdrop to the lawn. The administration pavilion encloses a garden court with public facilities at ground level. The restaurant bridges the lake and a footway connects the Loggia to the garden Amphitheatre, producing a variety of walks around the lake.

# Melanie Sainsbury Associates

Title———Entrance to "Service World"
Material—colour photocopy, line drawing, paper, ink wash
Size———280×420mm

Title———View of 'Service World'
Material—colour photocopy, line drawing, paper, ink wash
Size———280×420mm

This project was commissioned by the BBC to illustrate architectural proposals for the spaces under and around the "Spaghetti Junction" motorway intersection on the M6 in Birmingham.
At the moment a traveller is not aware of the spaghetti of roads that lie beneath him, nor of his close proximity to the city of Birmingham.
My project suggested a petrol station below the roundabout at Salford Circus, a tri-level of huts, food stalls and superloos known as the "Service World" which would provide for the traveller 24 hours a day, a 90 bedroom Motel on the river Tame, and a canalside street of bars, pool halls and cafes. The main thrust of the proposal is to link the world of the traveller to the city of Birmingham.

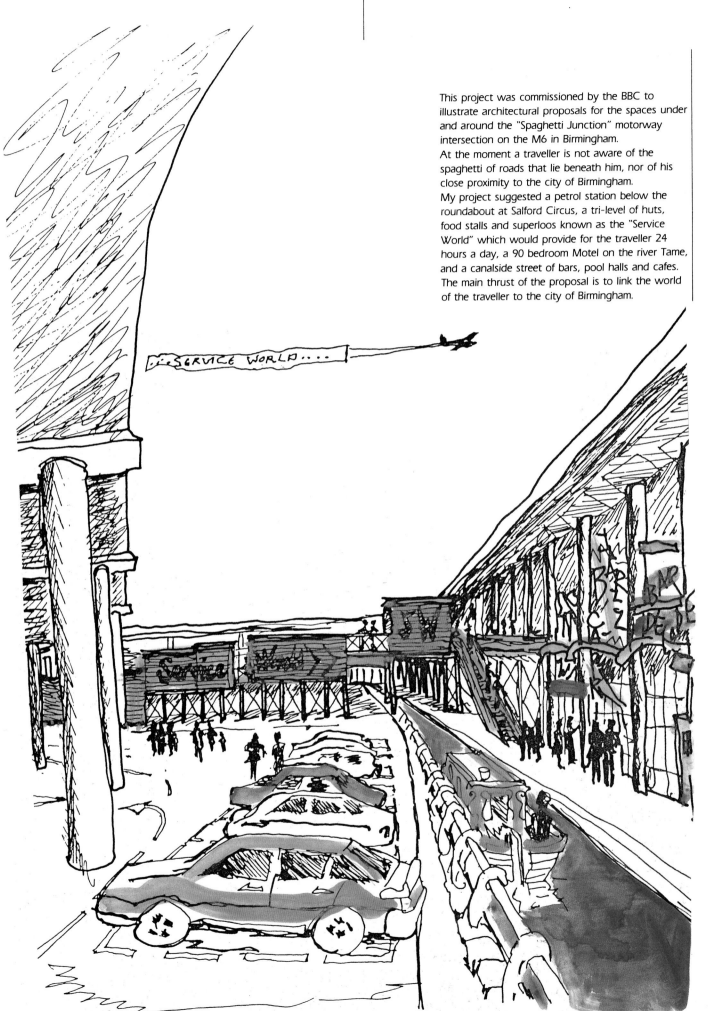

# Johnathon Sergison

Title———Porto
Material—ink, tracing paper
Size———594×841mm

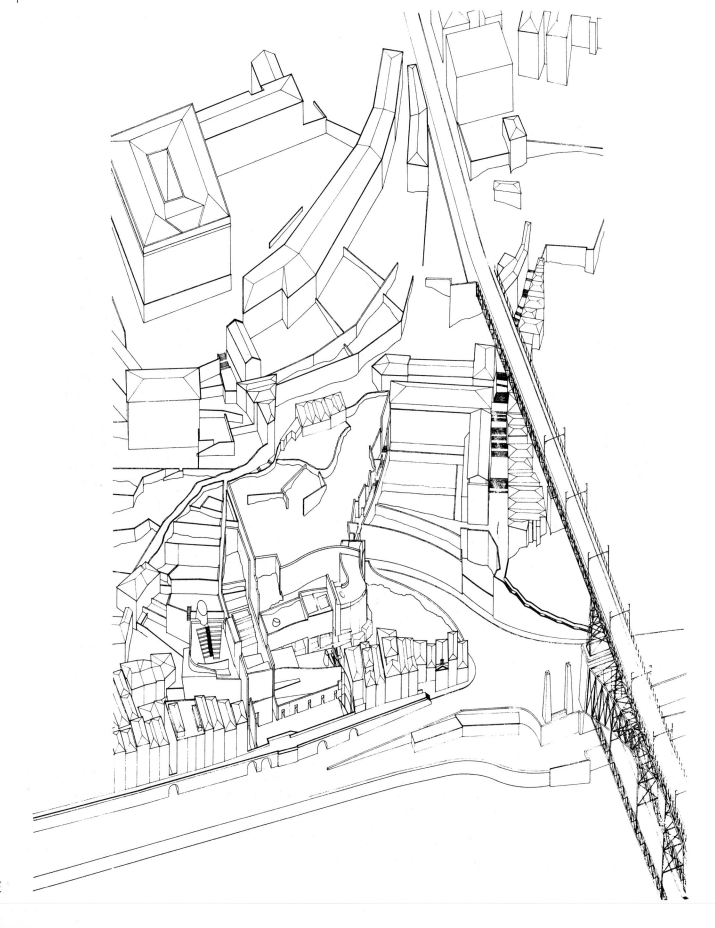

Title———Porto
Material—ink, charcoal, photocopy
Size———594×841mm

Situated under the Acropolis of the Palace and the Cathedral buildings, addressing the Duoro river and overshadowed by the nineteenth century Eittal bridge, this site is the missing link in the continuity of the city's elevation. It is my wish to create a sense of buildings which complete the facade of the city with materials that respond to those existing, but in an architectural language that is of this century. The very nature of the site demands a system of terracing to create habitable spaces. A middle ground is established between the cathedral square and the public square at the bottom of the site, where any intervention is kept to a minimum.

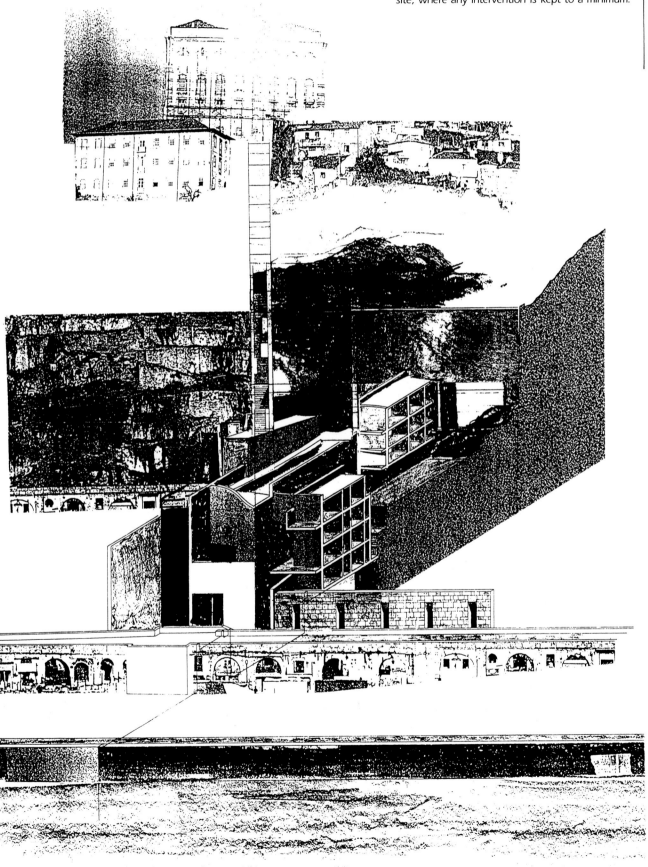

# Doug Patterson

Title———Maharajah's Palace, Mysore, India
Material—watercolour, colour pencils
Size———1000×900mm

To travel, draw and try to understand the
architecture of past civilisations, always
remembering the sagacious reflection by Paul
Vallery; "all arts live on the world and every work
demands a response".

Title———Fort Rock Temple, Trichy, India
Material—watercolour, graphite
Size———1100×950mm

Title———Kings Cross Station, London
Material—watercolour, colour pencils
Size———1200×1000mm

# Kay Ngee Tan With
# Christopher McCarthy

Title———A Green Square for a Grey City
Material—pen, pencils, pencil crayon
Size———420×594mm(each)

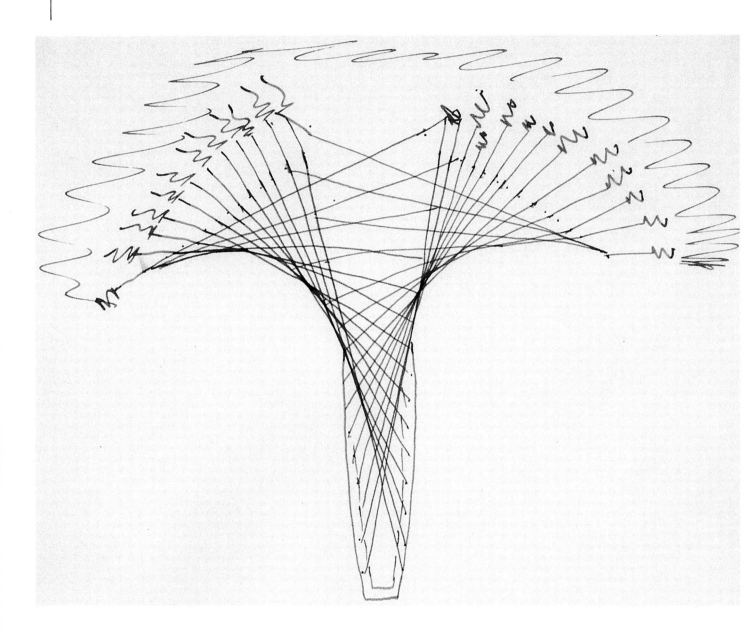

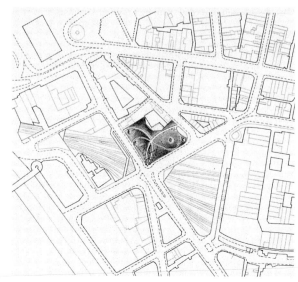

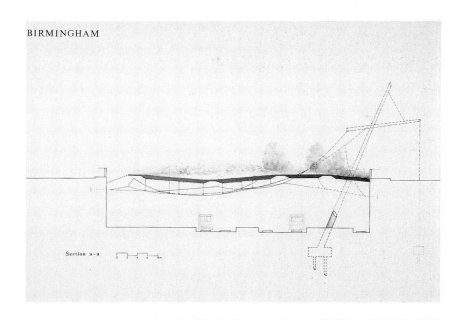

Section a-a

The Green Square which covers over a railway void gently stretches out to invite in pedestrians from all sides. Since it is surrounded by the busy, rushing traffic of Central Birmingham, the Square provides a moment of calm and peace for those who pass through.

The main structure is a net of cables, stretching to the four corners, which not only supports the garden fabric above but also allows the continuous flow of trains to occur underneath.

At some points the cables penetrate through the pre-cast garden cladding and top soil, expressing the beauty of the structural system in the garden above. The main masts signal an entrance to the square which also minimises the number of interruptions on the railway platforms below.

The distinctively bold appearance of the cable structure is designed to contrast and compliment the curvy and fluid pattern of the seventeenth century-like landscaping.

The heavy soil of the garden will be an effective acoustic barrier between the passing trains and the garden. At the perimeter there are openings which permit air ventilation for the platforms.

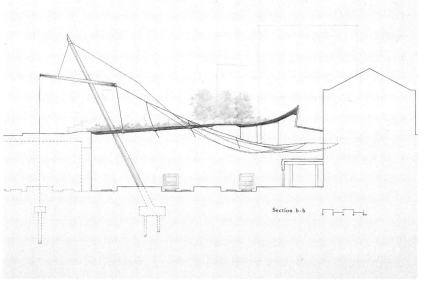

Section b-b

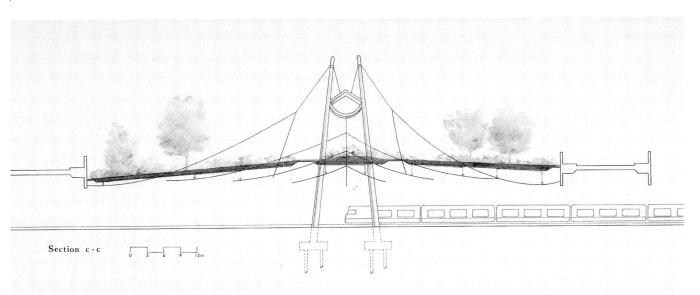

Section c-c

0    3    6    9    12m

# Peter Mance

Title———Electro-Acoustic Music Research Institute &
        Concert Hall, Auditorium
Material—80gm detail paper, graphite pencil, ink, chalks
Size———594×415mm

This project was envisaged to extend the scope of cultural activities on London's South Bank, to provide a self-contained centre of electro-acoustic music research, education and performance.

A new block is built to enclose the site and form an internal courtyard.

Three new vertical cores of circulation rise through the building, pierce the roof and landmark public access, define routes and focus vistas through the building.

The Edwardian shell is preserved and an acoustically isolated series of boxes are introduced (to form composer workstations of recording studio standard) on their own secondary structure within the fabric of the building.

These interventions aim to be musical and lyrical. They imply movement, dialogue and exchange as is fitting to any institute that solicits public awareness and involvement.

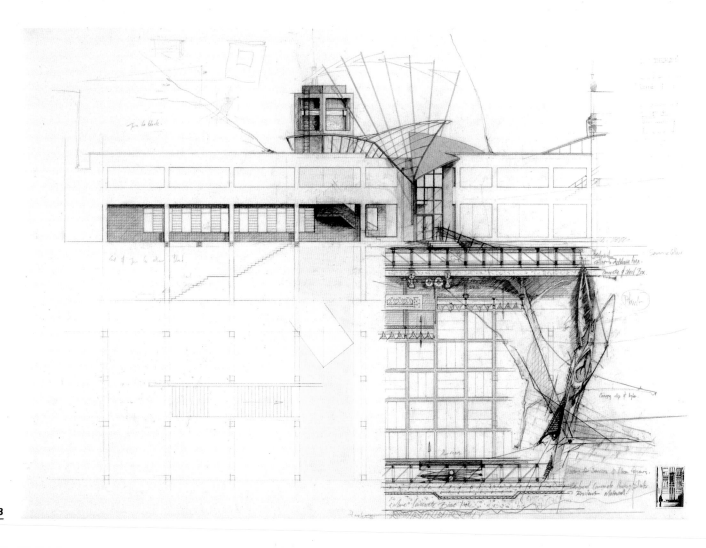

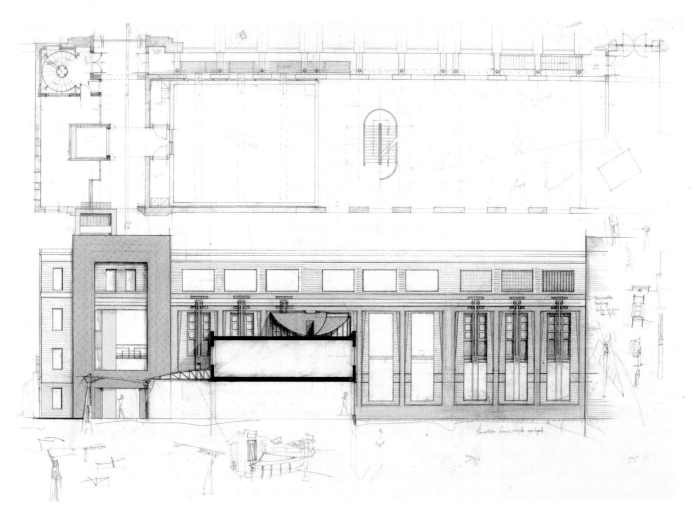

Title——Electro-Acoustic Music Research Institute &
           Concert Hall, Composer Study Block
Material—80gm detail paper, graphite pencil, ink, chalks,
           correction fluid(white)
Size——594×415mm

Title——Electro-Acoustic Music Research Institute &
           Concert Hall, Circulation Study
Material—80gm detail paper, graphite pencil, ink, chalks
Size——594×415mm

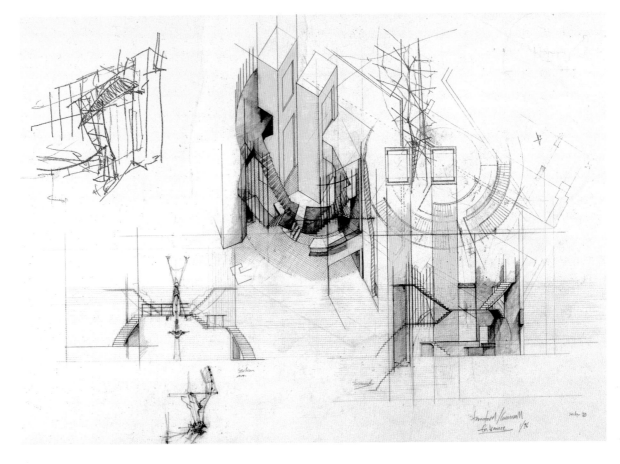

Title———Urban Park, Study Views of Axis Route and
             Incidents
Material—sketch paper, felt tip pen
Size———200×130mm See attached

To provide a series of sensory cells, to invite
pedestrians to pause and recover their sense of
environment. An anechoic wall suppresses the
bustle of traffic, a reflective wall reflects the
movement of clouds, nylon filaments sway in the
wind like tall grass, and small singular cells provide a
cloak for individual privacy and calm.

Title———Harbour Lighthouse Study
Material—80gm detail paper, graphite pencil
Size———595×415mm

# Louisa Hutton/
# Matthias Sauerbruch Architects

Title——————Aston Science Park, Birmingham, City Context
Material—ink, acrylic, film
Size————————420×200mm

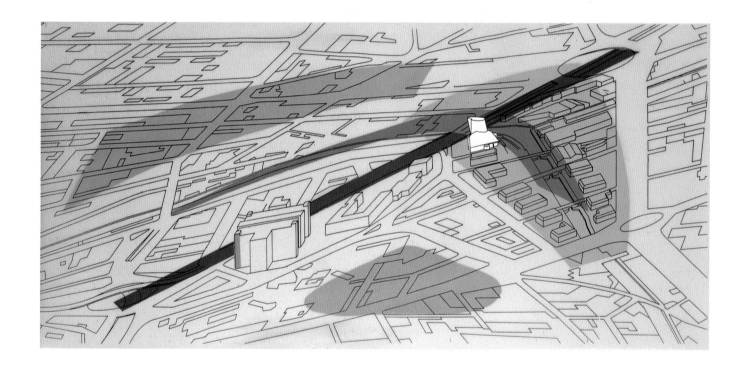

The project was for an International competition
("Birmingham Good Design Initiative") and gained
third prize.
Whilst providing a laboratory building with
associated offices to act as a "flagship" building for
the whole Science Park, we aimed to simultaneously
address the contradictory site conditions of an
urban motorway and a neglected and redundant
canal.

Title————Aston Science Park, Birmingham,
　　　　　Motorway Approach
Material—ink, acrylic, film
Size————420×295mm

Title————Aston Science Park, Birmingham, Canal Walk
Material—ink, acrylic, film
Size————420×230mm

Our proposal for the above-named competition provides a generous roof park on top of the "Mountain", with all the public facilities in its associated "Screen", whilst the more private conference halls and rooms inhabit the mountain as the places between a continued grid of city blocks.

Title——Tokyo International Forum,
　　　　The Mountain and the Screen
Material—film, ink
Size——594×841mm

Title——Tokyo International Forum,
　　　　City Arcadia
Material—film, ink
Size——594×841mm

Title——Tokyo International Forum,
          Conference Cascade
Material—film, ink
Size——420×594mm

Title——Tokyo International Forum,
          Hall A Interior
Material—film, ink
Size——420×594mm

Title——Tokyo International Forum,
          View From a Passing Train
Material—film and ink
Size——120×680mm

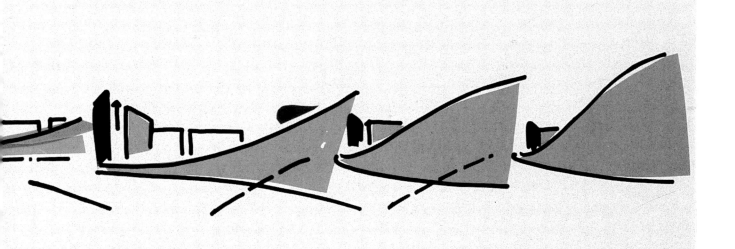

# Rik Nijs

Title——Waterloo Competition, Time of History-Time
          of Remembrance, Lethe
Material—ink, oil paint, goldleaf, film.
Size——420×594mm

The two collages serve as the first reaction to the brief and the site; 'The Fall of Icarus' and the gates of Hougoumont Farm. Both are intended to summon up the concept of allowing the farmers to get on with their ploughing. The conflicting walls of different materials serve firstly as a boundary which establishes a divide between culture and nature, and secondly they represent the still of the day after the battle and form, likewise, a haven of remembrance. The extended space between, functioning as a museum and physically experienced as a cleft, a cavern, a crypt or a grave, is a profane sanctuary dedicated to the vast numbers of forgotten dead.

Title——Waterloo Competition, Plans and Sections of
        the Inner Walls
Material—oil paint, linen canvas
Size——860×560mm

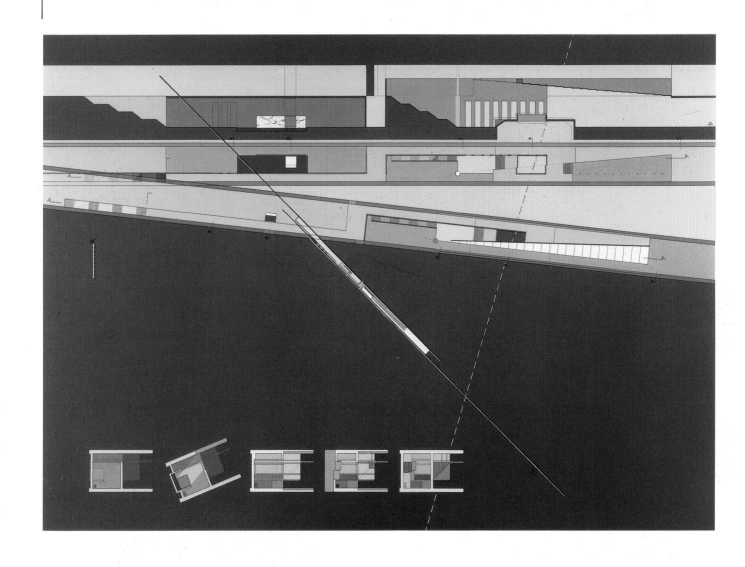

Title——Waterloo Competition, Plans and Sections of
        the Inner Walls
Material—oil paint, linen canvas
Size——880×560mm

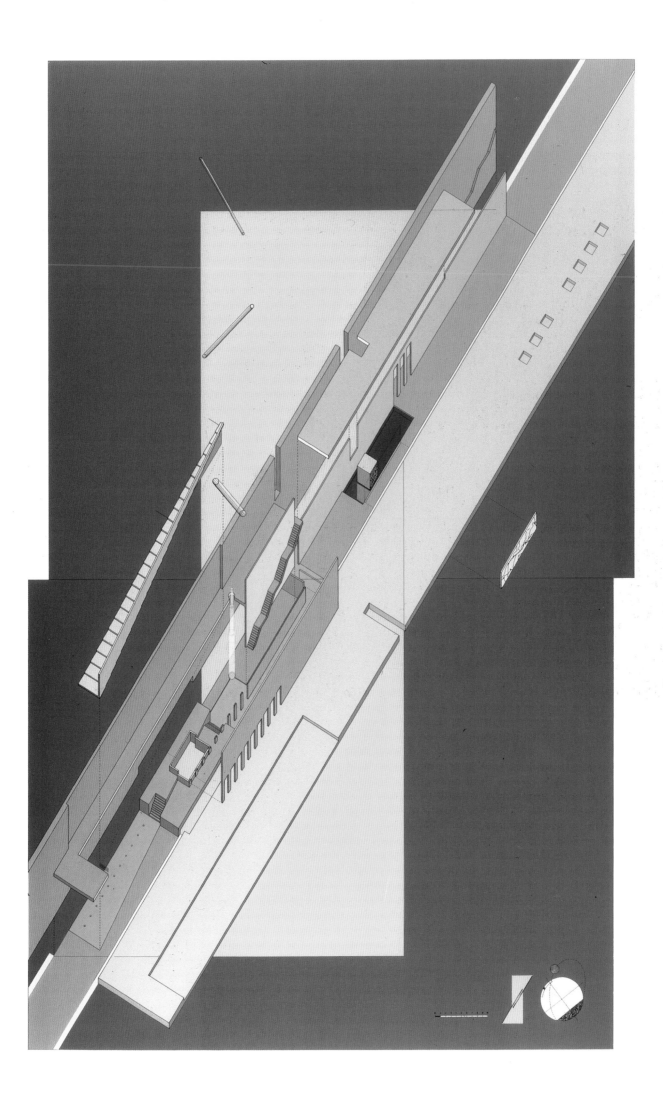

# Tim Ronalds Architects

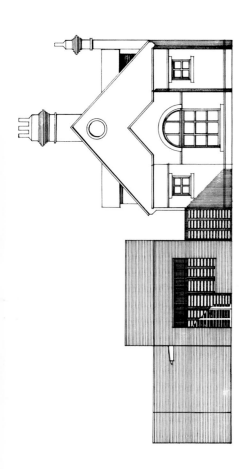

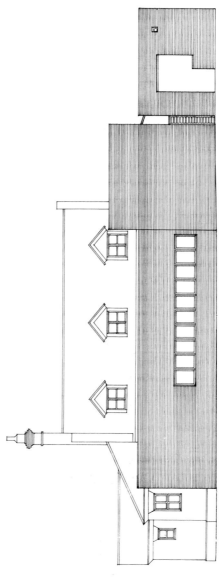

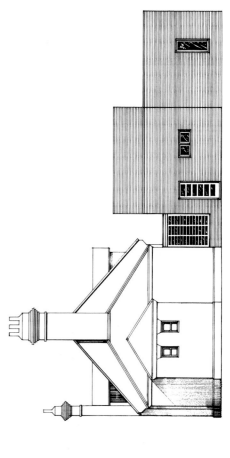

Title——Coroners Court Extension, Walthamstow, London
Material—ink, tracing
Size——297×420mm(each)

A small extension to a Victorian Coroners Court situated in the grounds of a cemetery next to a morgue. The programme required new arrival and waiting spaces for the public, and offices and service spaces for the staff. The building creates a measured sequence of spaces, top-lit and austere, which rely on light and volume to guide the public through to the courtroom. The essence of the design is the juxtaposition of a new language with an old. The materials are red brick and dark oak. The detailing is restrained and taut. It provides a natural dignity for the circumstances of death.

# Pawson & Silvestrin

Title——————Holiday Villa
Material—white crayon, black canford
Size——————297×420mm(each)

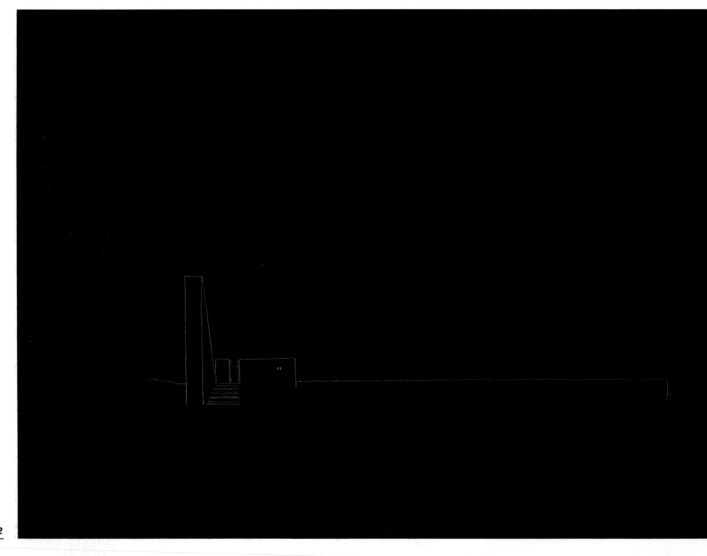

Title——————Holiday Villa
Material—white crayon, black canford
Size——————297×420mm(each)

A vertical gap (8×0.83metres) pierces the facade to draw the viewer into the atrium, a void-cube within a cube of massed walls. Sunlight and vistas of the surrounding landscape are "framed" by "frameless" small windows.

Exterior walls are rendered in local brown-reddish soil. Floors and fixed furniture are of local quarry stone. The long narrow pool (3×40metres) projects from the terrace's step towards the horizon ending as a water-fall. Rooms are generous in space, hardly furnished and cell-like. The minimum number of elements belonging to the house's "gestalt" construct a place of solidity, fortification and calm, liberating the see-er from the memories of the metropolis.

# Pierre D'Avione Architects

Title——— "Room in the City", Office Installation for
        International Linen Palazzo Stelline, Milan
Material—ink, tracing paper, acrylic paint, colour pencil,
        ozalux paint
Size——— 594×841mm

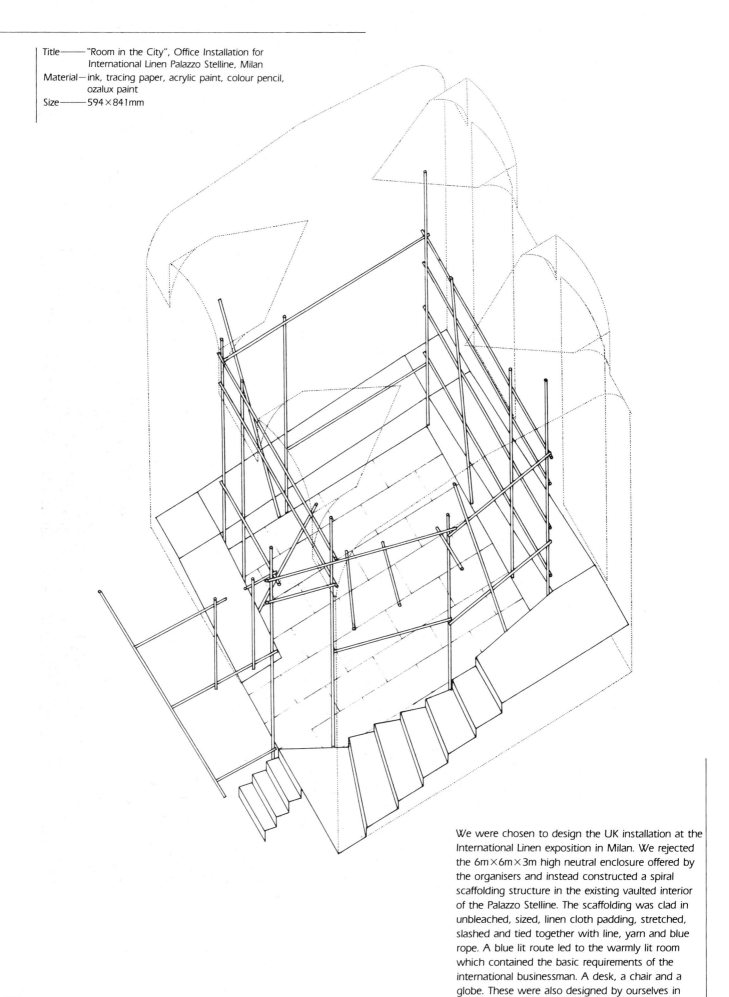

We were chosen to design the UK installation at the International Linen exposition in Milan. We rejected the 6m×6m×3m high neutral enclosure offered by the organisers and instead constructed a spiral scaffolding structure in the existing vaulted interior of the Palazzo Stelline. The scaffolding was clad in unbleached, sized, linen cloth padding, stretched, slashed and tied together with line, yarn and blue rope. A blue lit route led to the warmly lit room which contained the basic requirements of the international businessman. A desk, a chair and a globe. These were also designed by ourselves in wenge and linen moire.

Title——"Room in the City", Office Installation for
  International Linen Palazzo Stelline, Milan
Material—ink, tracing paper, acrylic paint, colour pencil,
  ozalux paint
Size——594×841mm

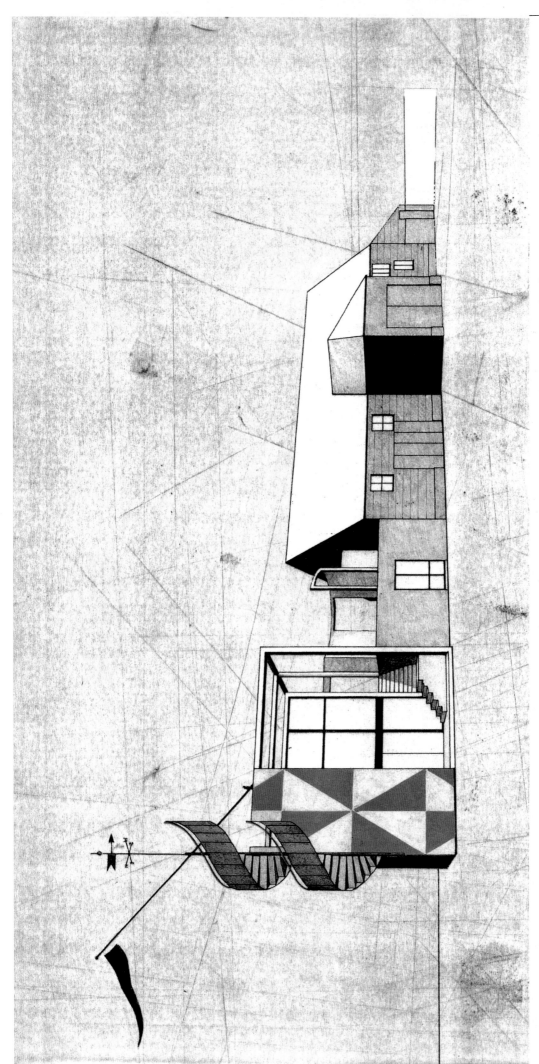

Conversion and extension of an existing barn by the Thames for the *Walton Society*. The barn is to be used for performances and the extension to provide an entrance, box office and bar at ground level, and a studio/outdoor performance on the first floor.
The new building acts as gatehouse to the site which will be used for future art-related development of the site.
The new building is timber framed and clad in plywood to be used as an advertising hoarding for the arts centre.

Title——Walton Arts Centre, Surrey, England
Material——ink, photocopy, colour pencil, paper
Size——210×420mm

# Terry Farrell & Company Ltd.

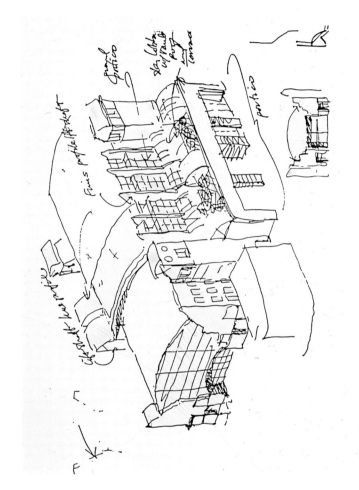

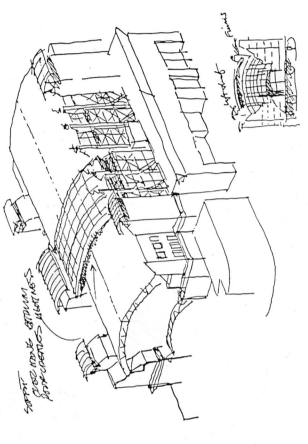

Title——Embankment Place, Urban Project, London
Material—colour pencil drawings
Size——210×297mm

In recent years high land values in London have made the most impossible sites potentially profitable. This project, above Charing Cross railway station, echoes the vault of the station's original roof, long since destroyed, and makes a confident contribution to the eventful Thames skyline. Of equal importance to the main block are the improvements to its surroundings. The station forecourt, Villiers Street, which runs down the north side of the station, and the adjoining Embankment Gardens are all currently neglected and tatty spaces; Farrell's scheme will restore and repair them, and draw them into a larger piece of urban design. At the same time the vaults underneath the station will become a new world, reminiscent of the lower half of Tobacco Dock, composed of shops, bars and the reinstatement of a theatre which formerly occupied the site. "Architecture & Urbanism (A+U)'89/12 104 Pg."

Title———Embankment Place, Urban Project, London
Material—ink, trace
Size———210×297mm

Title———Embankment Place, Urban Project, London
Material—ink, trace
Size———210×297mm

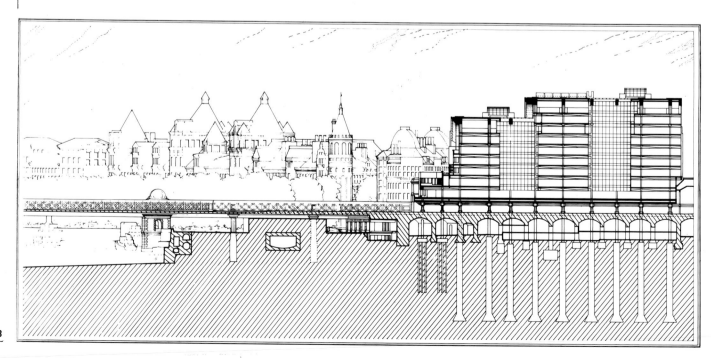

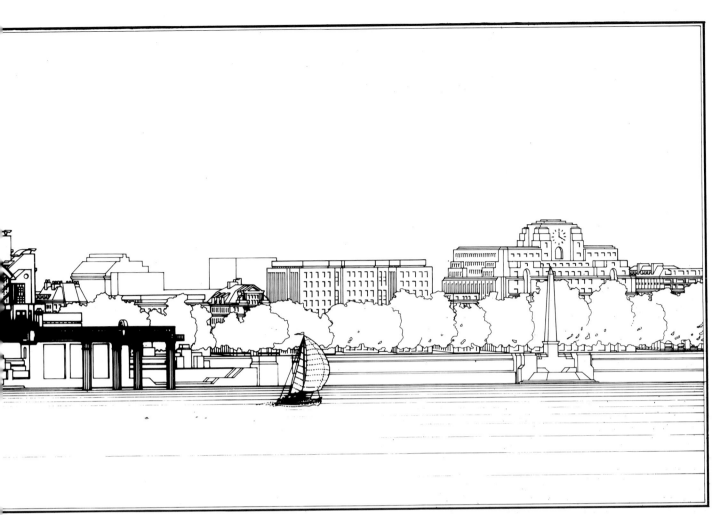

Title———Embankment Place, Urban Project, London
Material—ink, trace
Size———210×297mm

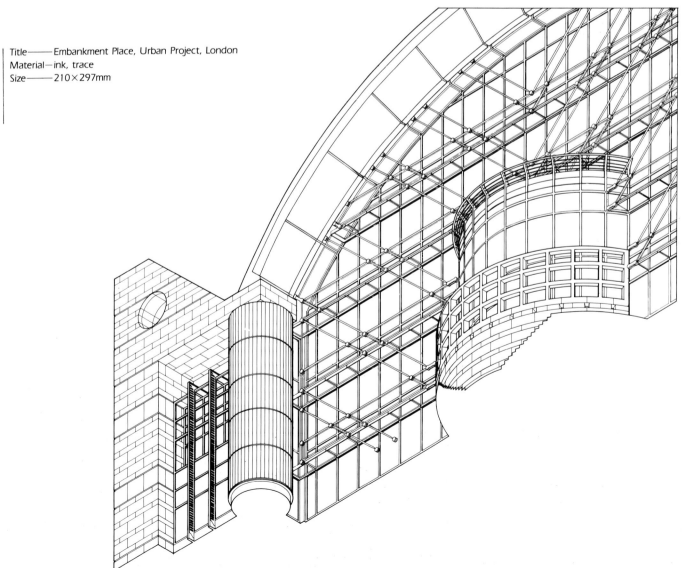

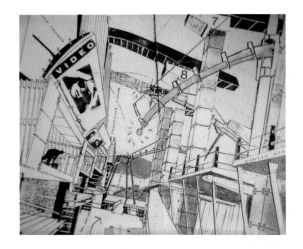
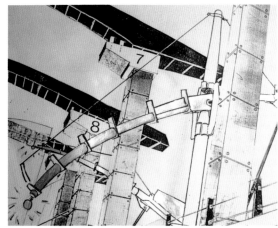

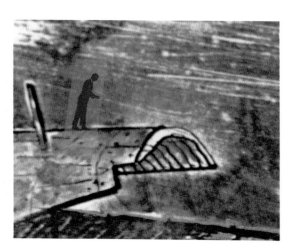

Title———Play-in-house
Material—oil pastel, acrylics, paper
Size———210×295mm(each)

Title———Play-in-house
Material—ink, collage, film
Size———830×580mm

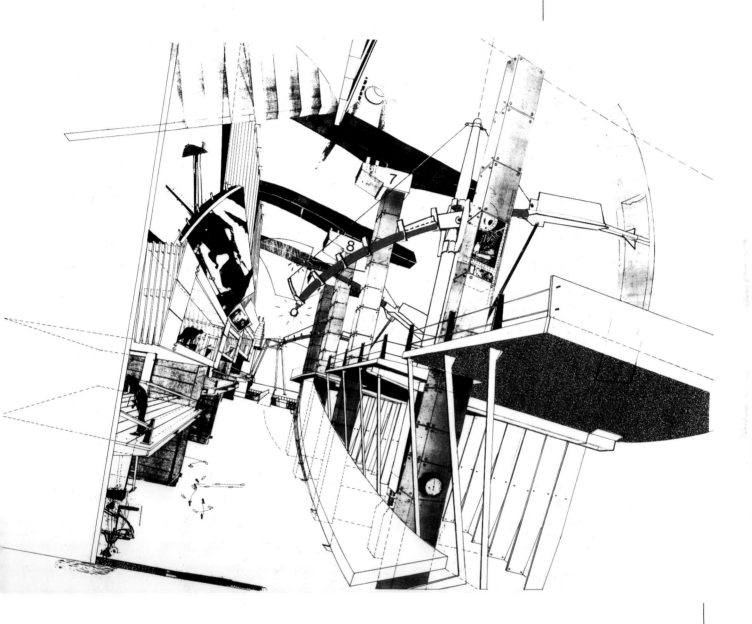

The contemporary performance space is something that lies between the "street" and the "room". The Playhouse becomes the Play-in-house as much as the theatre of the street becomes the (street of) theatre. The overlapping events of performer/spectator recall the instantaneous ambiguity of street disorder. Stages (rehearsing) as room containers similar to large television sets of continuous action (the city never sleeps).
The drawing reverberates back at the spectator, through the collection of disjointed objects, events and surfaces, as our gaze is reflected when we look at goods in a shop-window: the inner surface of surrounding space, a section of space (inwards) and that of transgressing its limits (outwards).

# Mark Pimlott

Title——London Project
Material—ink, paper
Size——420×297mm

Title——London Project
Material—ink, paper
Size——420×297mm

# Tony Fretton Architects

Title——Mute Records
Material—ink, tracing paper, transtext photomontage
Size——841×594mm

I had felt for a long time that there was poetry in this type of building which could be brought out with thought, and this was my chance.
I aimed to use the same or similar materials as were in the building, and to reuse as much of the existing building as possible, partly for the sake of economy, but mainly to prove it is the state of mind of the designer that makes the design a joy, not necessarily his material. I am sure that this is not unconditionally true, and I have not since had the opportunity to discover these conditions, but this is still an area that fascinates me.

Title——The Lisson Gallery, London
Material—ink, tracing paper
Size——841×594mm

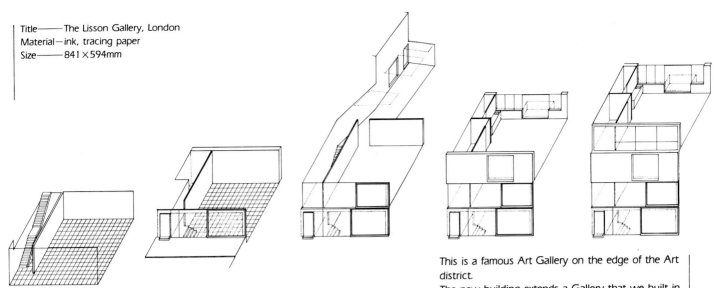

This is a famous Art Gallery on the edge of the Art district.

The new building extends a Gallery that we built in 1986, but although it touches the former building, it is only linked in one part, and has its own address, which because the site goes around a corner is different.

In this way it can provide a quiet space for new young artists, or for single experimental pieces by established artists, away from comparison with the bigger existing gallery.

Each room is 7m×7m×3.5m high, a single space on each floor with a staircase at the side as in an atelier.

The ground and first floors are glass from floor to ceiling, so that where the floorboards stop the street begins.

From the outside the building is half like a building and half like a rack on which the artists are invited to place their works right up against the street.

The link to the existing building is beautiful, toplit and serenely unattended, as is the new gallery itself, so that when visitors attend as they do singly or just in pairs, they have the possession of the whole of the space and great intimacy with the works on show.

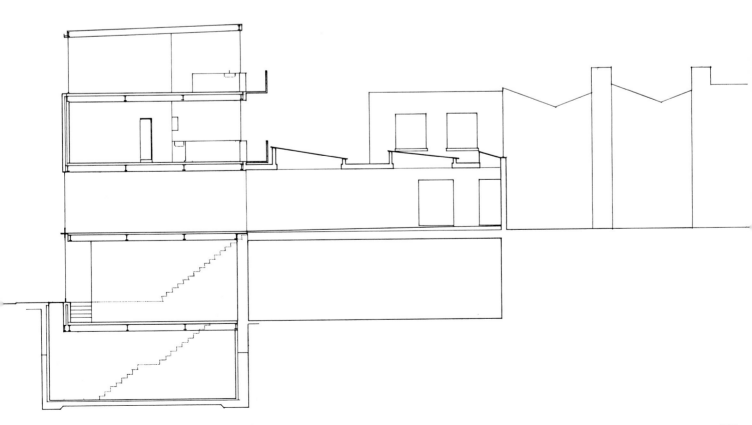

# Peter Sabara

Title——Buy, Buy Banking-exploding View
Material—trace, pencil, ink, wax crayon
Size——1800×840mm

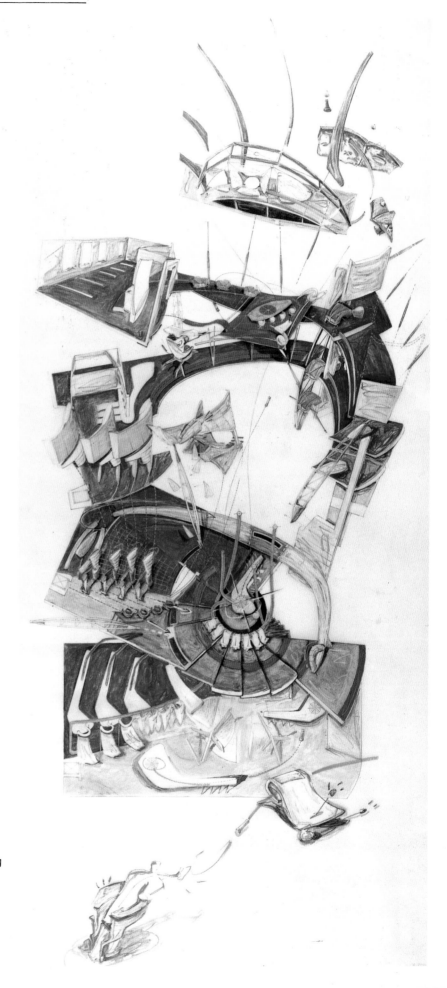

This project proposes a new public interface with the high street bank by fusing the disparate events of saving and gambling into a demonstrative trading floor with a "hands on" approach to using it. Pneumatic tubes whisk commodities up from the vaults below. A backdrop of auto mated cashiers and customised car dashboards, line the rear of the building - providing computerised banking services with video link-up to similar banks throughout the city. These tiers act as observers' galleries to the spectacle below.

| Title——— | Brixton Emporium, Section |
| Material— | trace, pencil, oil pastel, spray paint |
| Size——— | 940×590mm |

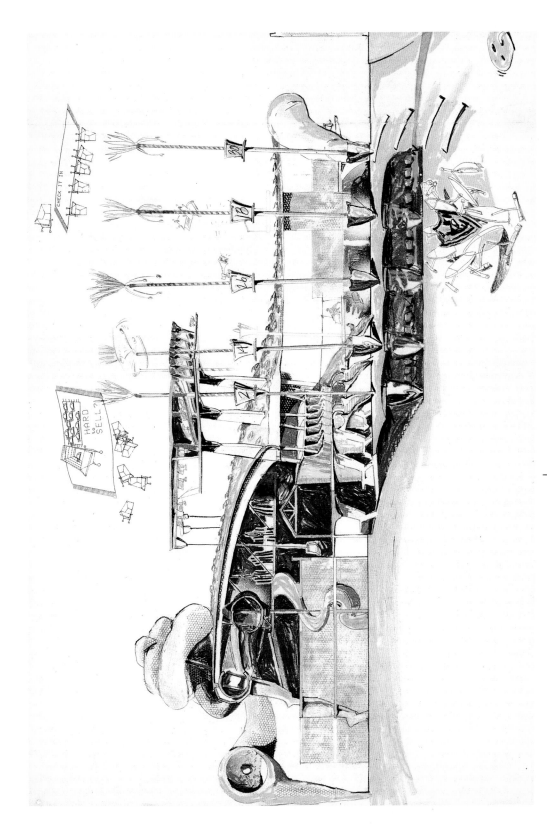

In the "hard-sell" world of trading, subtlety is lost on the viewer, so architecture can be hyper-expressive of the events it accommodates. The organic roof which vaults over the existing buildings, is built up of discarded appliances such as irons and radios embedded in concrete; the building doubles as an advertisement for the market for second-hand goods and spare parts below. Above, existing wig shops are accommodated inside a palatial turban form. Opera boxes offer a view from the existing arcade onto the sales pitch.

# Wickham & Associates Architects

This house is situated on the island of Easdale some fifteen miles south of Oban on the west coast of Scotland. The village is formed around a large green with lines of cottages arranged close together to afford protection from the wind, and the new house is located across the green from the small harbour.

The project was commissioned following a fire which destroyed the former house, and the brief included the retention of the original four walls and pyramidal roof. It has been constructed on a concrete base upon which stands a stout timber frame supporting the roof. The walls are of stone and concrete blocks and the roof is of local slate with steel eaves and gutters to protect the top of the walls below.

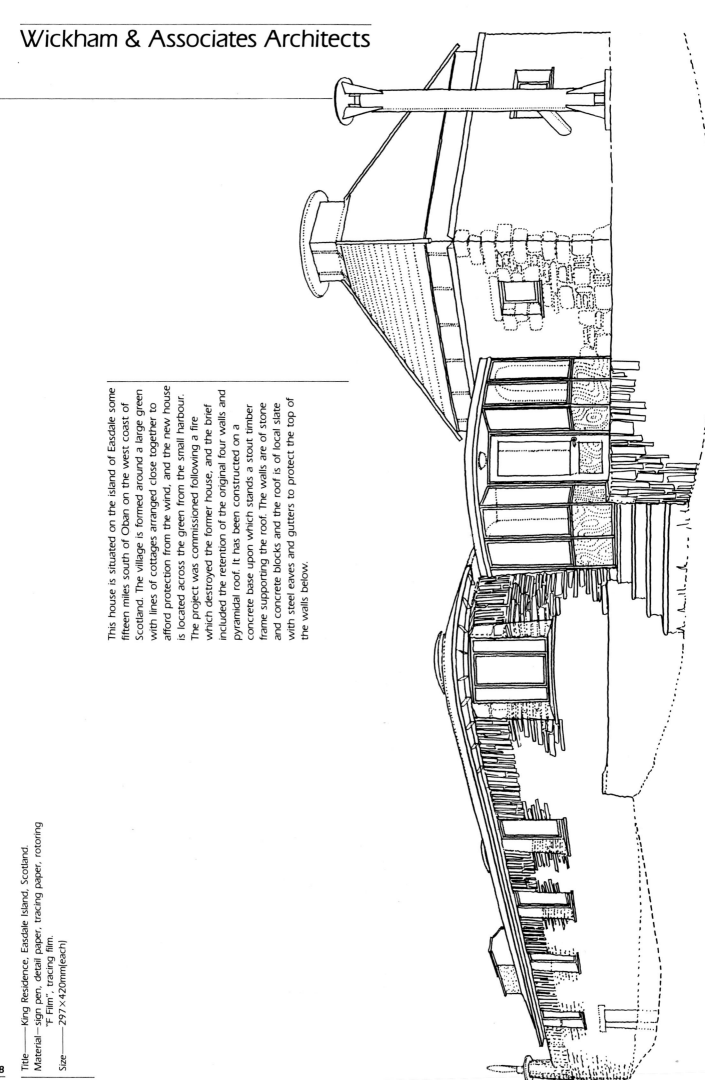

Title——King Residence, Easdale Island, Scotland.

Material—sign pen, detail paper, tracing paper, rotoring "F Film", tracing film.

Size——297×420mm(each)

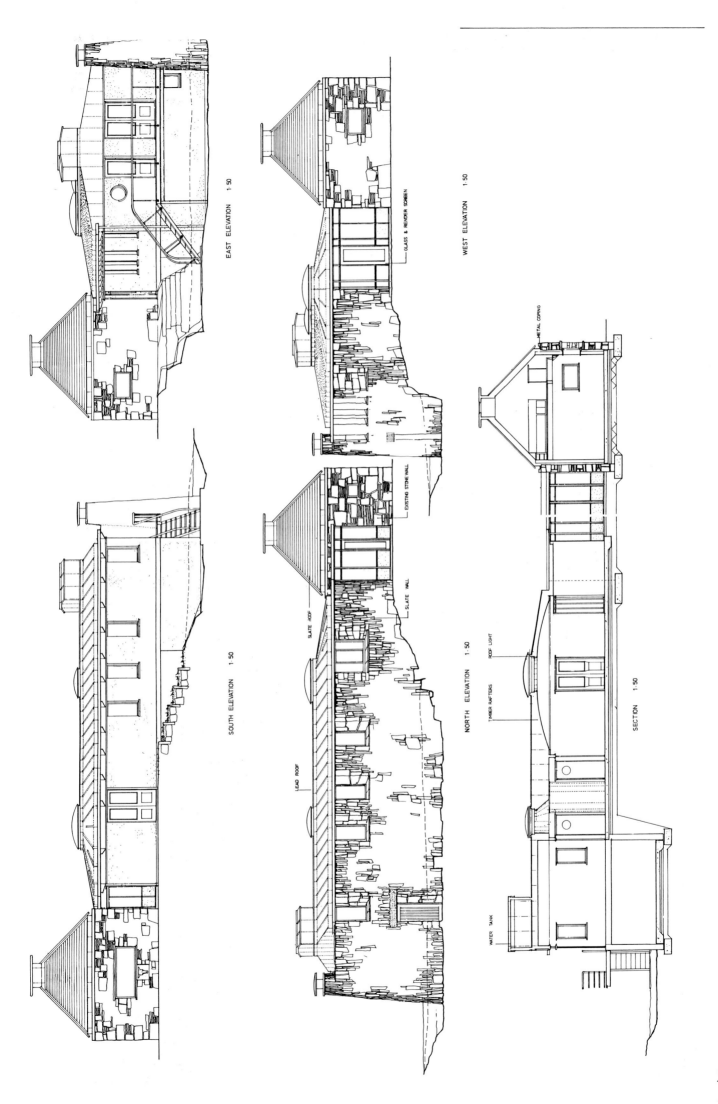

EAST ELEVATION 1:50

WEST ELEVATION 1:50

GLASS & RENDER SCREEN

SOUTH ELEVATION 1:50

NORTH ELEVATION 1:50

SLATE ROOF

LEAD ROOF

EXISTING STONE WALL

SLATE WALL

SECTION 1:50

METAL COPING

ROOF LIGHT

TIMBER RAFTERS

WATER TANK

# Kevin Rhowbotham

Title———Rosyth Plus-Ultra
Material—gold, ink, graphite, pastel, gauche.
Size———950×2850mm

Modernism's characterisation of tectonic space as
instrumental — as space to be used for something
— generates a functionalist mapping of spacial
possibilities, and privileges a categorical, unequivocal
representation of its object.
The superimpositional flux of events, of actions
played out simultaneously in space and time, is
overlooked by architectural drawing practice, in
favour of the pseudo - mimetic, instrumentally
representational nature of the generic sketch or
presentation drawing.
Rosyth Plus-Ultra avoids this categorical figuration
by superimposing alternative, contradictory even
layered images of its fictional object, simultaneously,
as a sum-collage.

Title———Perseus Plus-Ultra
Material—crayon, pastel, ink, gauche, graphite
Size———400×950mm

ANALOGY ". . . the judgement 'good' does not originate with those to whom 'goodness' is shown! It is rather 'the good' themselves, that is to say the noble, powerful, higher placed and high-minded, who felt and posited themselves and their actions as good, namely as of the first rank, in antithesis to everything low minded, common and plebian. (Conversely) The free human being is immoral because in all things he is determined to depend upon himself and not on a tradition: in all the original conditions of mankind, 'evil' signifies the same as 'individual', 'free', 'capricious', 'unusual', 'unforseen', 'incalculable'.

There is nowadays a fundamentally false theory of morality which is especially celebrated in England: according to this theory the judgements 'good' and 'evil' are the summation of the experiences of 'useful' and 'not useful'; that which is called 'good' is that which preserves the species, that which is 'evil' is that which injuries the species. In truth, however, the evil impulses are just as useful, indispensable and preservative of the species as the good: only their function is different." Concept. . .
Verfremdung/EVIL

Title——Limehouse Zero
Material—transfer, ink, pastel
Size——375×980mm

Architectural theory, conceiving the city as a
material figure, operates a primary fallacy which is
structural to the legitimacy of its operation vis, that
life takes place primarily in SPACE. Bergson's
spacialisation of time and Proust's privileging of
inadvertant memories, focus on the act of
re-membering as the animator of consciousness.
From this point consciousness IS memory and the
object "space", outside time, ceases to exist in the
qualitative realm.
Limehouse Zero explores the possibilities of
SIMULTANEITY.
Contexts and drawing styles are deliberately
superimposed to encourage a simultaneous reading
in the single image.
It makes play with the categorical sketch.

# Powell-Tuck Connor+Orefelt Ltd.

Title———Interior of Vittoriale - House of Pleasure,
　　　　　Roppongi, Tokyo
Material—pencil, acrylic paint, oil pastel
Size———1000×1000mm

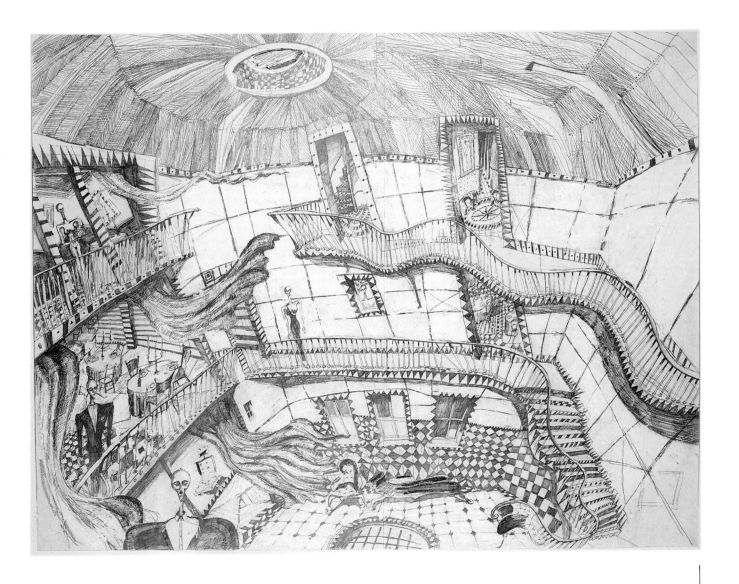

A new building containing a nightclub, French and Italian restaurant. The concept was to make a total entertainment complex in which to spend the entire evening. The imagery is distorted and surreal. The picture shows the main interior space.

Title———Graphic Design Studio - Venice, California
Material—pencil, oil paint, acrylic paint, oil pastel
Size———1000×1000mm

The construction of a new studio is an addition to an existing garage. The main studio space is lit by small windows to the south and a larger one to the north-west.

# Simon Conder Associates

Title———Unitarian Square Development
Material—water colour, cartridge paper
Size———480×380mm

The design of a new office buiding on a historic site in the center of Ipswich. The project also involves the restoration of existing properties, the construction of a small infill building and the creation of two landscaped pedestrian squares.

The project was to design a new lifeboat and
coastguard station on the seafront at Lyme Regis.
The design was one of the commended entries.

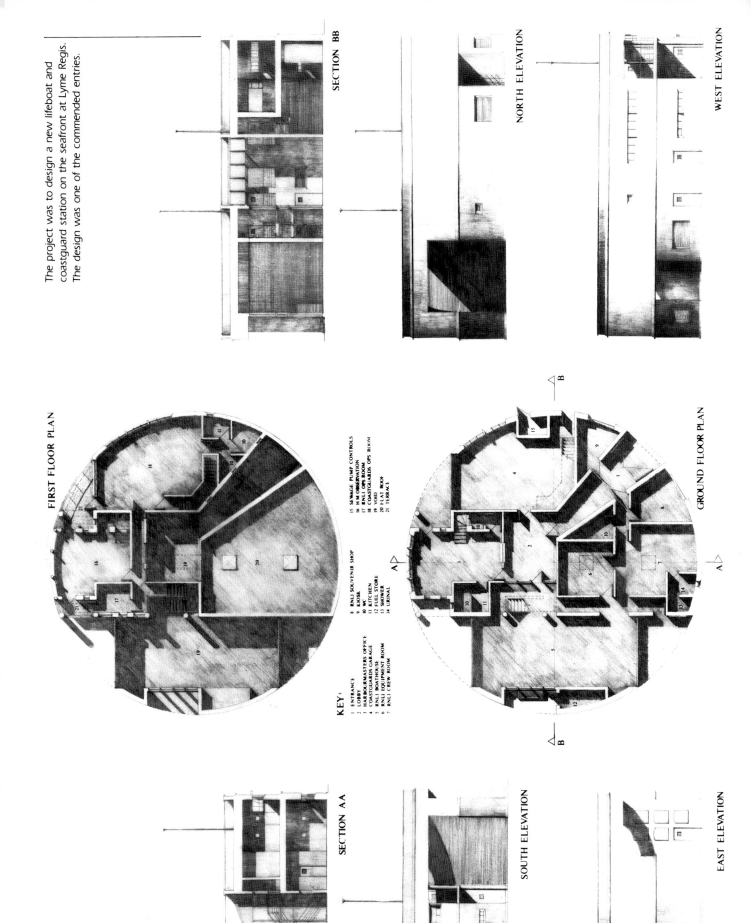

SECTION BB

NORTH ELEVATION

WEST ELEVATION

FIRST FLOOR PLAN

GROUND FLOOR PLAN

SECTION AA

SOUTH ELEVATION

EAST ELEVATION

KEY:

1  ENTRANCE
2  LOBBY
3  HARBOURMASTERS OFFICE
4  COASTGUARDS GARAGE
5  RNLI BOATHOUSE
6  RNLI EQUIPMENT ROOM
7  RNLI CREW ROOM

8  RNLI SOUVENIR SHOP
9  KIOSK
10 WC
11 KITCHEN
12 FUEL STORE
13 SHOWER
14 URINAL

15 SEWAGE PUMP CONTROLS
16 HM OBSERVATION
17 RNLI OPS ROOM
18 COASTGUARDS OPS ROOM
19 VOID
20 FLAT ROOF
21 TERRACE

Title——Lyme Regis Slipway
Material—pencil, tracing paper
Size——840×600mm

# Trevor Horne Architects

Title——Stables Mongewell Park
Material—ink, photocopy, trace
Size——230×530mm(each)

The stables are designed as an Object in the Landscape. It is a microcosm of the whole estate with a triangular walled compound containing the stable pavilion. Large roofs sail over the wall - as troughs to collect water and as baffles to reflect light onto the courtyard.

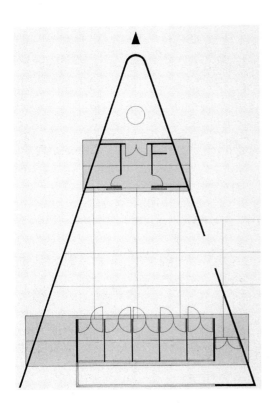

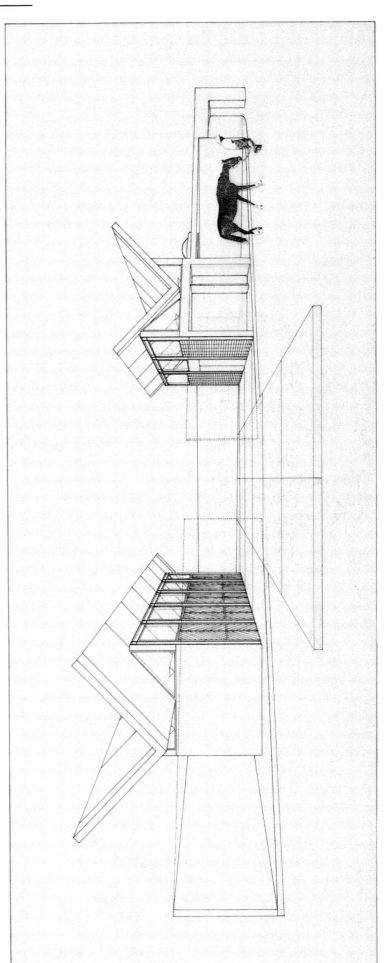

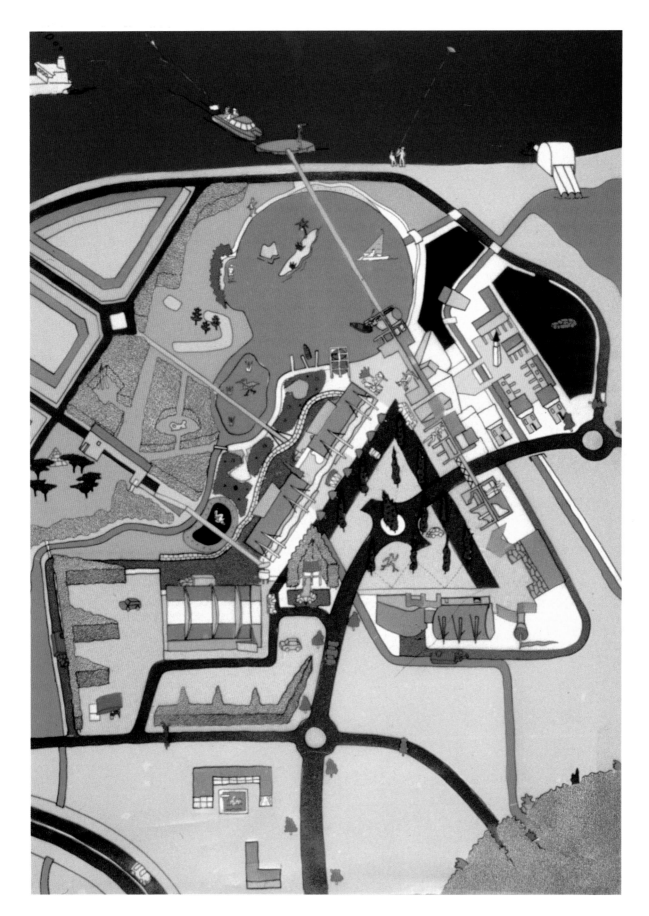

Title———Thamesmead - Clockwork
         Orange
Material—pantone, pen, plastic film
Size———590×765mm

The scheme creates an urban form using sub-urban type large retail "sheds", large leisure "sheds" and a gigantic Superstore (200k.) - a modern hybrid of the city. To these ingredients were added a series of civic uses. Our strategy was to create a "collage" by placing in juxtaposition the various elements of civic, retail and recreational activities so creating a varied texture of use. Each of these elements is given a public face around a triangular place - the point of arrival for one thousand five hundred cars.

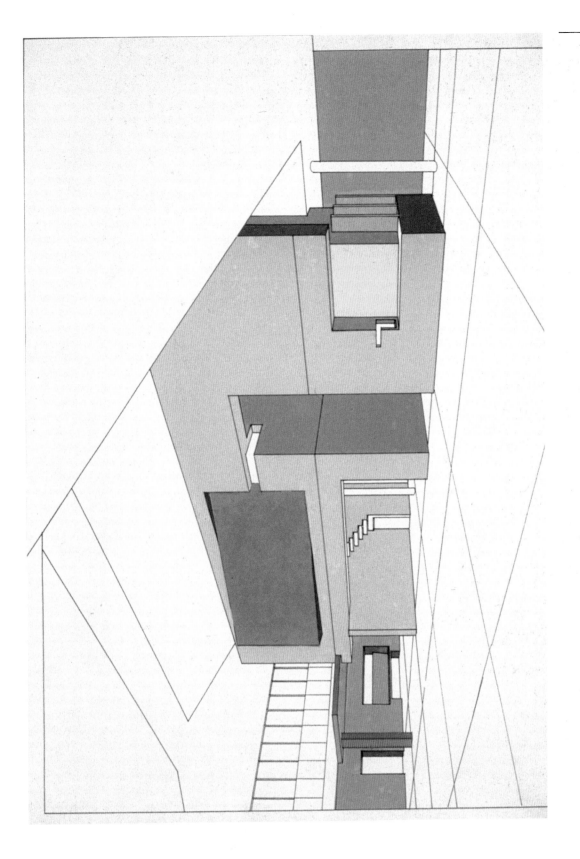

Title——London Hospital
Material—ink, film, pantone colour
Size——320×230mm

The main installation, a large wall, in the existing space forms the new structuring element. The wall houses the shops below and hanging from it is the large new signboard. Suspended from the wall is a canopy denoting the restaurant while above and within the wall is a place for the porters - an Inhabited Wall.

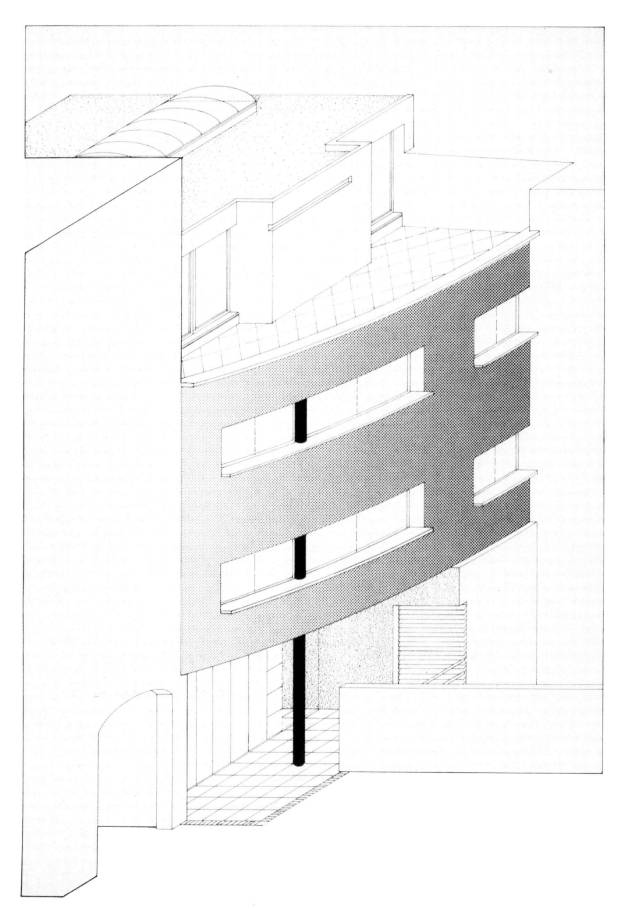

Title———Lisson Grove, Apartment
              Building
Material—ink, letratone, trace
Size———270×390mm

The scheme has three distinct programmes: office,
shop and residential. As to the apartments, the
street facade continues the formal Georgian terrace.
At the rear, as part of a mews, is the main entrance
to the apartments.
The main facade is an abstract screen hovering
above the porch giving the entrance shelter. This
new building terminates the rear courtyard and
contrasts with the existing haphazard order.

Title——Regents Park Road - Office Building
Material—ink, trace
Size——330×260mm

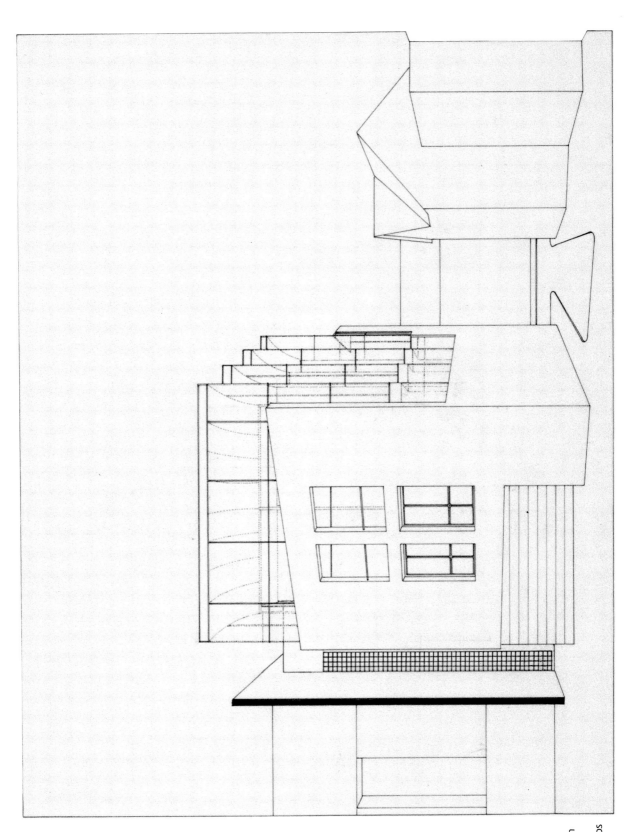

This project explores the notion of a building within a building. A brick screen, which continues and extends the language of the adjacent facades, wraps around a contemporary glass and metal volume.

# Martin Smith

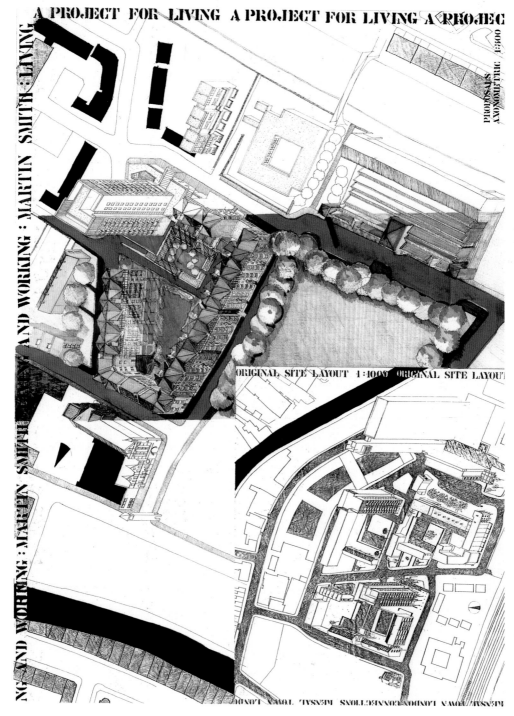

Title——Dissertation Project, Kensal Town, London
Material—ink, pencil, crayon, pantone pen, paper.
Size——597×840mm

The challenge of this project was to redefine the edges of an urban "island" in conjunction with others and to select sites for the creation of places in which to work and to live.

Historically the place to work and the place to live have experienced a marked distinction, but this must be challenged in the post-industrial world. In this scheme the sites are located around a public square. Each house unit comprises of seven apartments, the penthouse one being a studio/flat with large glazed areas creating a wall of light such as at the "Maison de Verre". The proposal for the workplace was for the creation of a bicycle factory located to the south of the square.

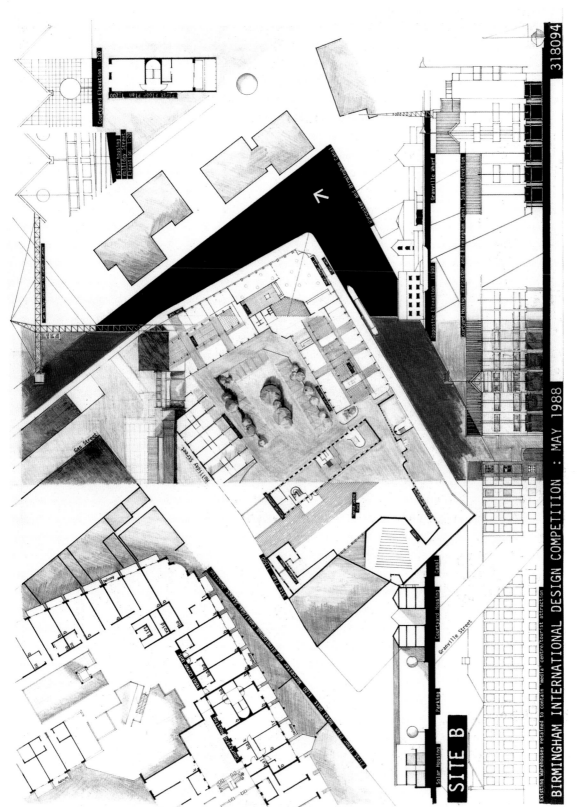

Title———Scheme for Birmingham Design Initiative

Material—ink, pencil, crayon, cartridge paper,
type face lettering.

Size———597×840mm

The scheme redefines the edges of the derelict site bounded on two sides by a canal. It is but a two minute walk from the new Convention Centre. Around the site there is a wealth of industrial buildings of archaeological importance: Birmingham was once the manufacturing heart of England.

This scheme attempts to address these buildings in both its new buildings, by setting up a thematic flow in the rhythm of the facade and by refurbishing two existing warehouses to the west of the site.

It is a mixed use scheme incorporating a hotel and restaurant at the junction of the canal, and by locating a media centre above, uses the lattice - like nature of the new transmission tower to declare a new type of technology by which this revival is taking place.

A further development would be to introduce the canal into the site, and in so doing create an island for car parking.

At the time of the petition, Birmingham, the UK's second largest city was undergoing a construction revival, and the symbol of the crane, utilised here was adopted by the author to symbolise this fact.

**183**

# Peter Thomas

Title —— Mecca Store - High Street Exchanges
Material —acrylic, mylar
Size —— 841×1189mm

Customers bound for the Meccastore from the tube stations do so without recourse to the street - a new traffic of ideas and intentions. Sales are divided into four arenas - clothing, leisure, finance and accessories. Customers choose from the sample commodities hung down from the retailers on the roof above the trading pits. Meccastore prices reflect supply and demand, rumour and quality, and their relative proximity to the high street and high finance, give rise to a "New Order of Public Trading"

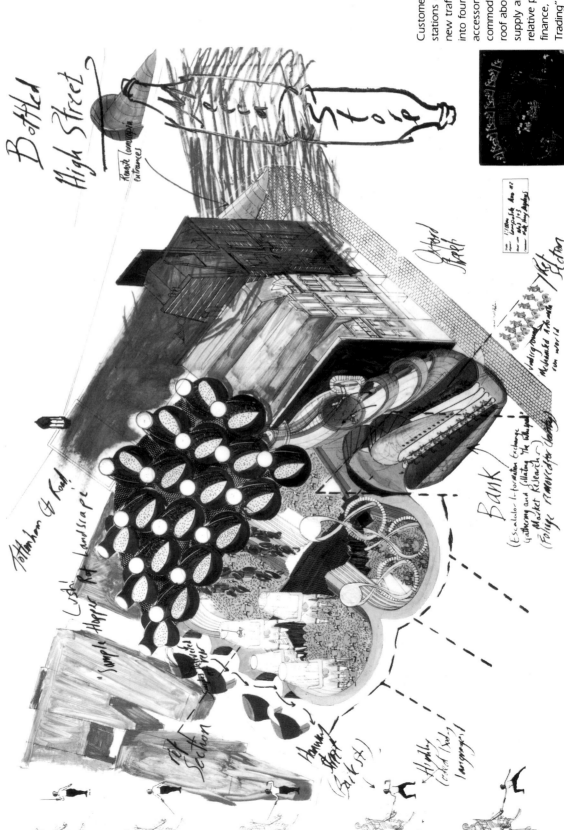

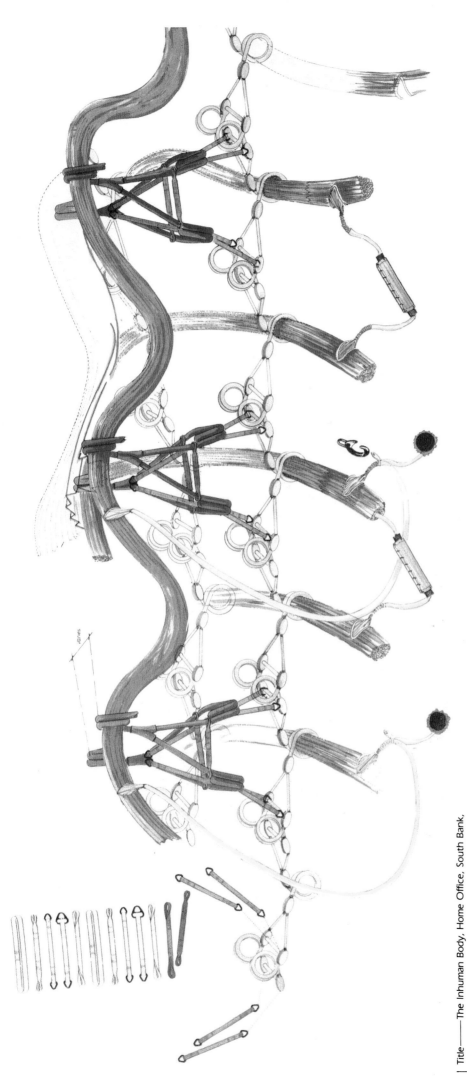

Title——— The Inhuman Body, Home Office, South Bank,
London

Material—acrylic, mylar

Size———420×594mm

The building is designed to move with the changing influx of people, to become a responsive indicator, architectural fabric here has become soft, fleshlike, with muscle and bone, an architecture that inhabits the world between the tensile and the compressive. The drawing shows the expansible roof. An arrangement of helical torsion springs devised to form extensible trusses under compression, and elasticated tie arrangement to work under tension.

# Stefano'De Martino

Title———City House Project.
Material—charcoal, paper
Size———410×290mm

Stretched over three back plots in a dense urban context, the City House establishes living conditions by "parking" elemental pieces which are the focus of each section: car pit/barbeque and pool; fireplace and wall bench; courtyard bedroom. Each fragment is independent, running on the cycle of its own rhythms, activities, associations; the simultaneous perception of all of them reveals a constantly changing unpredictable combination of experiences.

Title——Amphitheatre, Skyros, Greece
Material—charcoal, paper(each)
Size——230×175mm(each)

Part of a winning competition entry for the town of Skyros, suggestions were invited for the design and location of facilities for the community.

Here the amphitheatre occupies a natural bowl at the end of a valley that reaches into the centre of the village.

It amplifies the existing traces on the land: stone walls, terraces for farming, steps leading up/down the inclines.

The elements are there, and reinterpretation makes them visible. With minimal modifications the setting can be used for small-scale performances or larger events, or revert to its natural condition: accessible landscape.

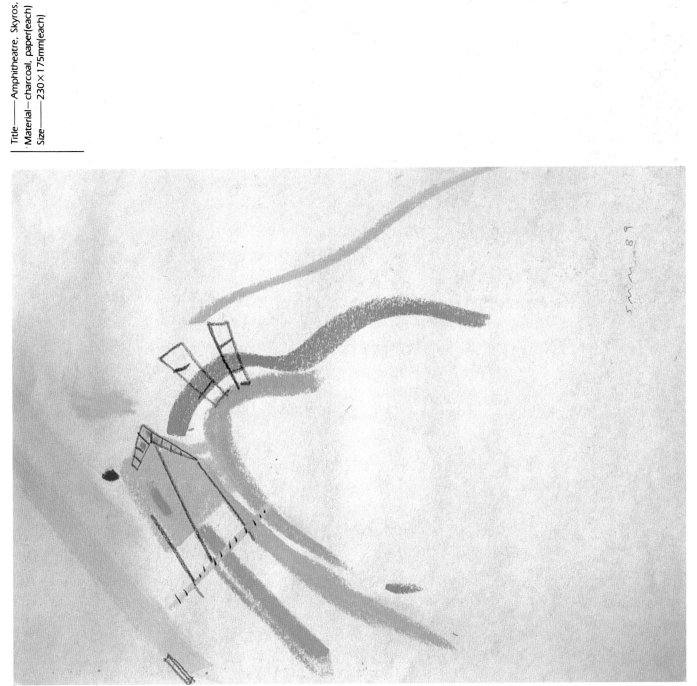

# Tom Heneghan With Inga Dagfinnsdottir

Title———The House with Blue Eyes
Material—etched screen photograph, felt tip, airbrush
Size———410×410mm(all)

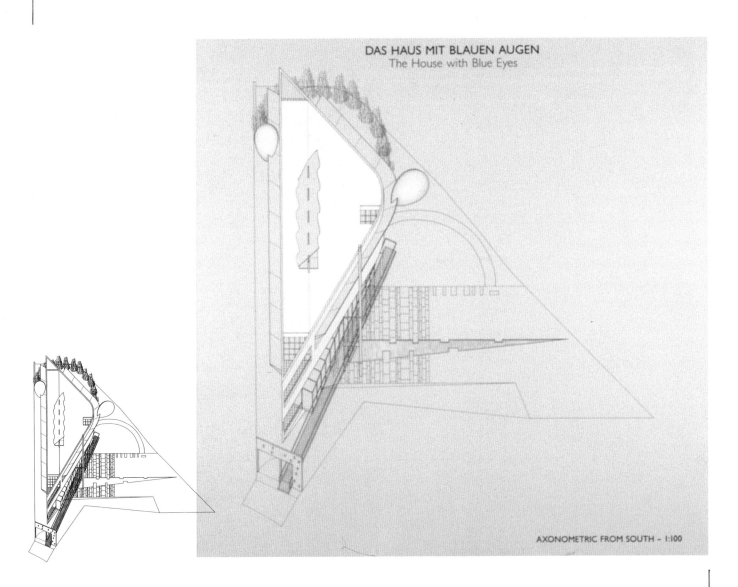

DAS HAUS MIT BLAUEN AUGEN
The House with Blue Eyes

AXONOMETRIC FROM SOUTH - 1:100

The house has "Blue Eyes", and a pale pink skin. It is approached through a steel screen gate, which is perforated with glass discs to refract light - indicating one of the characteristics of the house. The path is a flexible steel ramp bridge - the "softness" of the bridge reflects the difference between the "hard" public sidewalk and "soft" home territory.

The horizontality of the bridge is contrasted by the verticality of the tall living room which is extended by openings in the top floor which spill light down to the centre of the house from a rooflight above. Over the rooflight is a hinged reflector which tilts at mid-day to catch sunlight on either side of the house.

Reflecting light down into the private court and also into the garage driveway are the two "Blue Eyes" - with pliable mirror skins.

Above the bedroom windows are "visors" clad in stainless steel, which shade the windows from the high summer sun, reflect inward the low winter sun, and are used at night to bounce spotlights to give a "halo" of general illumination to the garden.

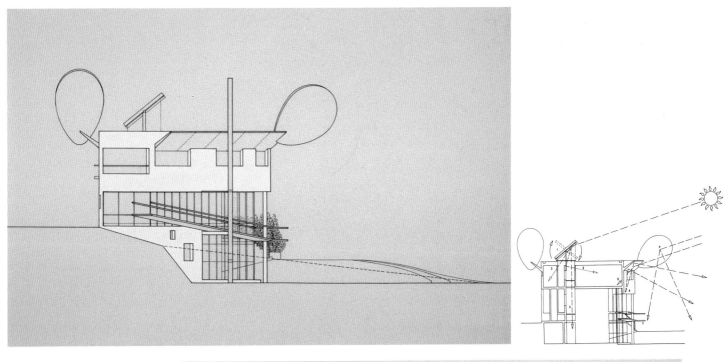

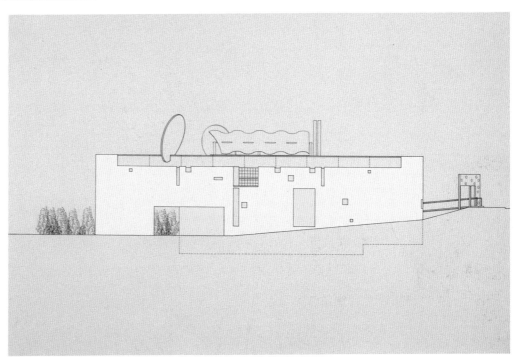

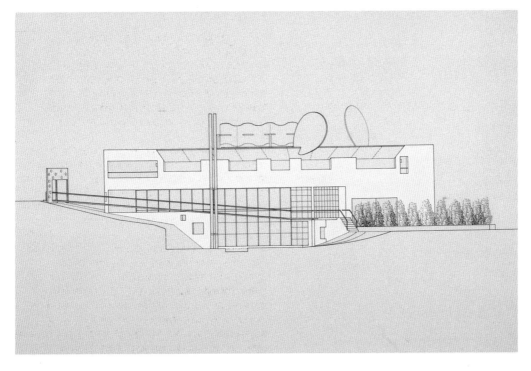

# Weil and Taylor

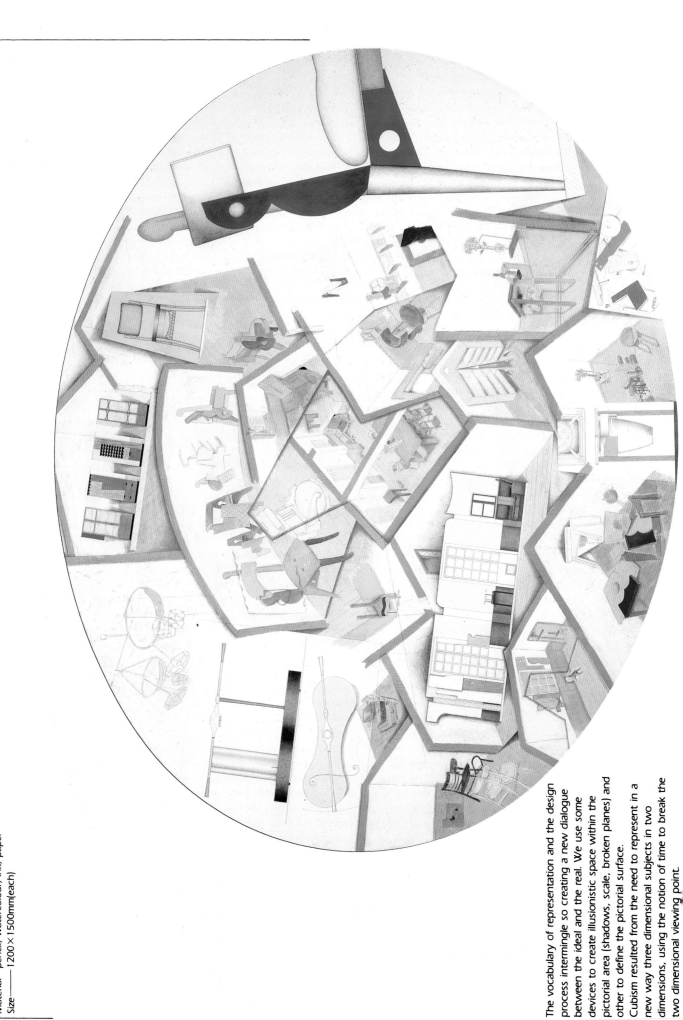

Title —— Living Room, No.1 Grosvenor Cottages
Material — pencil, watercolour, ink, paper
Size —— 1200 × 1500mm(each)

The vocabulary of representation and the design process intermingle so creating a new dialogue between the ideal and the real. We use some devices to create illusionistic space within the pictorial area (shadows, scale, broken planes) and other to define the pictorial surface.

Cubism resulted from the need to represent in a new way three dimensional subjects in two dimensions, using the notion of time to break the two dimensional viewing point.

We have used cubism and its convention as a metaphore for the design process that inhabits time. The design process has no pre-determined order or organisation. The creative result emerges at the end as a reading of a series of parts that together assemble into the whole.

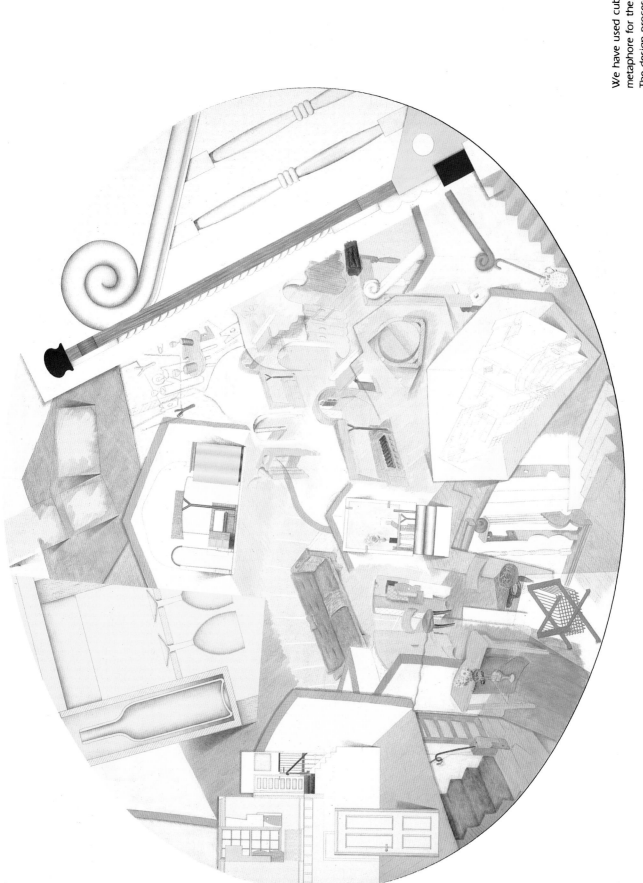

# Will Alsop & John Lyall
# Architects

Title———Tower Project, Herouville St. Clair, Normandy,
 France
Material—acrylic, canvas
Size———2500×1500mm(each)

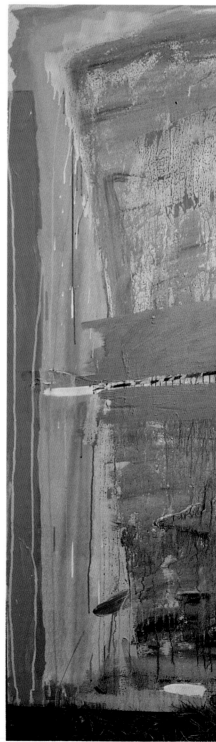

The concept for our part of the project was to introduce a link between the Centre Commerciale and L' Hotel de Ville. To make this more interesting we have introduced shops and an aviary. This should attract more people.

"I always use the medium of painting to generate architecture, but the paintings are large and you have to use your whole body to make the image. This is in direct contrast to the usual architect's 'thumb nail' sketch or back of the envelope job, which is often done on the train or while looking at the television. I want my sketches to be large enough to fill the whole of my perception and in this way I can discover the qualities of the emergent building".

# Williams & Hawley Architects

Title——The Summer Centre, Highgate, London
Material—letrafilm, tracing paper
Size——594×841mm

The Summer Centre is the home of the Summer Play Project, a local charitable foundation in Highgate, North London, which provides play facilities for children during the school holidays. Upon completion the centre will be made available to local residents, childminders, mother and toddler groups, pensioners and an After Schools Club. A new glazed entrance screen was positioned symmetrically opposite the original doors on the central axis of the building, and a hollowed out cylinder was positioned on this axis.

The activity rooms are square and well fenestrated to the front and rear with kitchen areas positioned to the rear. A new entrance gate in the existing garden wall provides access to a small walled garden and the centre.

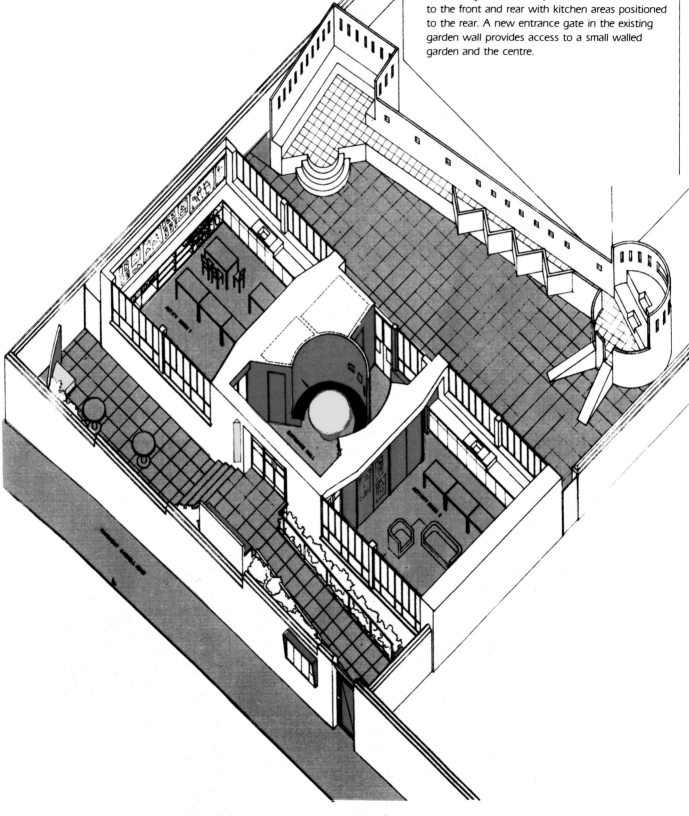

Title——————Conversion of Drawing Room Flat
               in Edinburgh's Georgian New Town.
Material—ink, tracing paper
Size——————594×841mm

Firth of Forth

Granton harbour

Botanical
gardens

Dean river

48 India St

Princes St

Castle

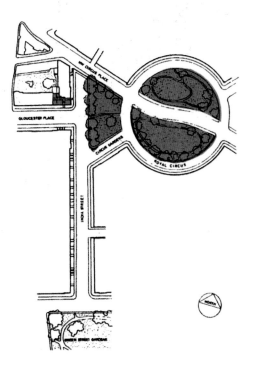

# Philip Michael Wolfson

Title———Gallery, Apartment Interior
Material—wk+coloured pencil, paper
Size———280×400mm

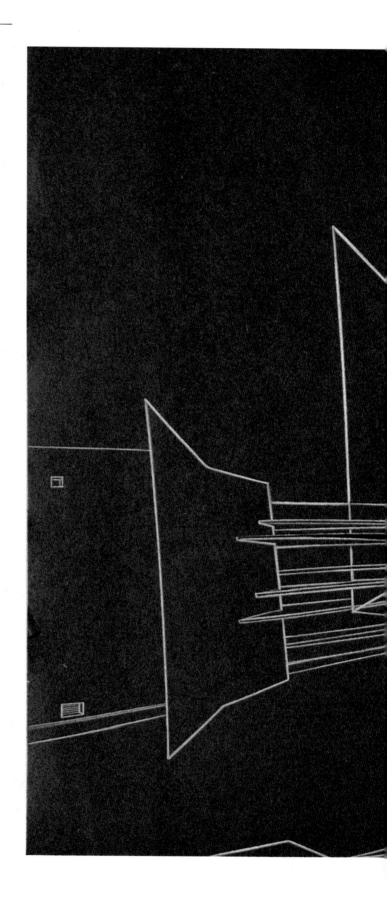

Conversion of a relatively small living space within
an apartment for use solely as a gallery of 20th
century decorative arts.
To insert a series of new walls and elements within
the existing framework of the room to fulfill all of
the fundamental requirements for storage and
display; to intensify a contrast of curve against linear
(existing) qualities of the space.

Title———Chair Study
Material—ink, drafting film
Size———280×400mm

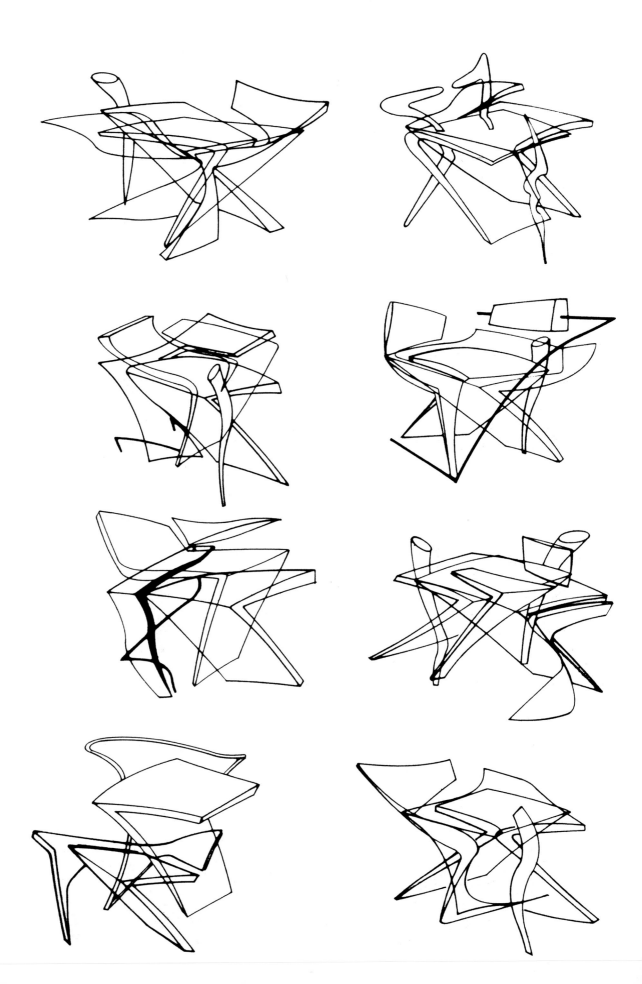

Fluid versus fixed geometries (or dynamics) was the
initial idea behind the approach to this study.
The drawing itself serves as a means of developing
various ideas specifically concerning the supports
and the backs of the chair which was to be
designed for a restaurant in Sapporo.

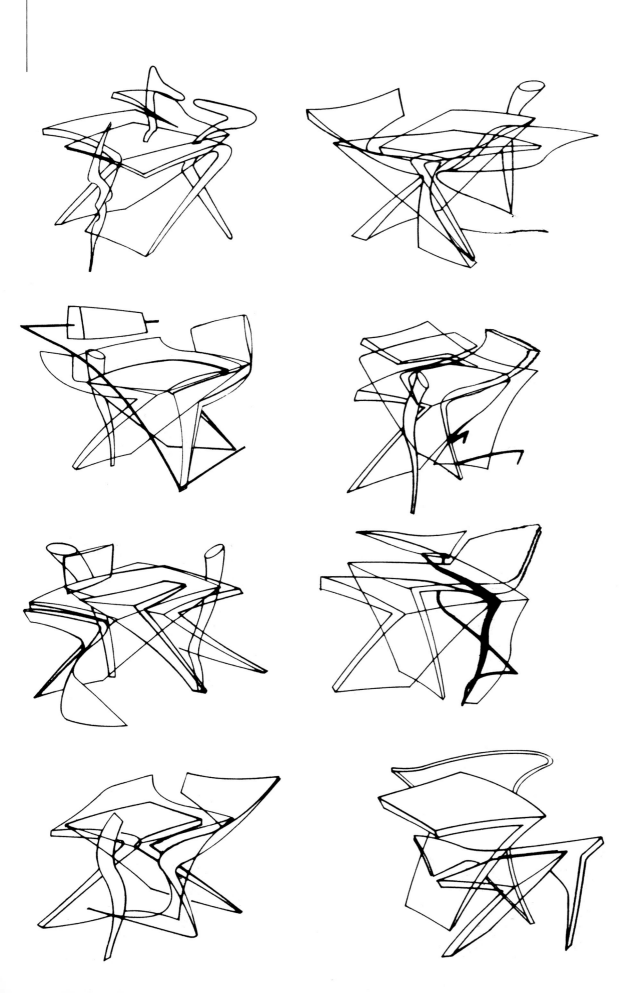

# Troughton McAslan

Title———St.Peters Street
Material—ink, tracing paper
Size———594×841mm

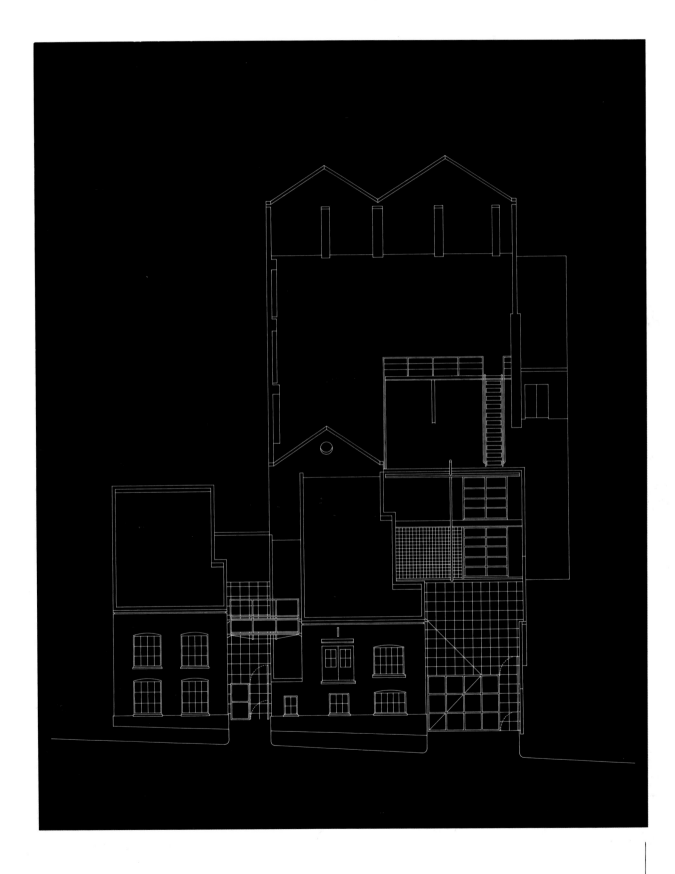

Planometric drawing showing the alterations which
we proposed for the building and which have now
been carried out.

An aerial perspective sketch of our proposals. We were third prize winner in this open competition for the urban design regeneration for the centre of Edinburgh in Scotland, and in particular the valley which separates the New Town from the Old Town.

Title———Waverley Competition
Material—felt pen, draft paper
Size———420×594mm

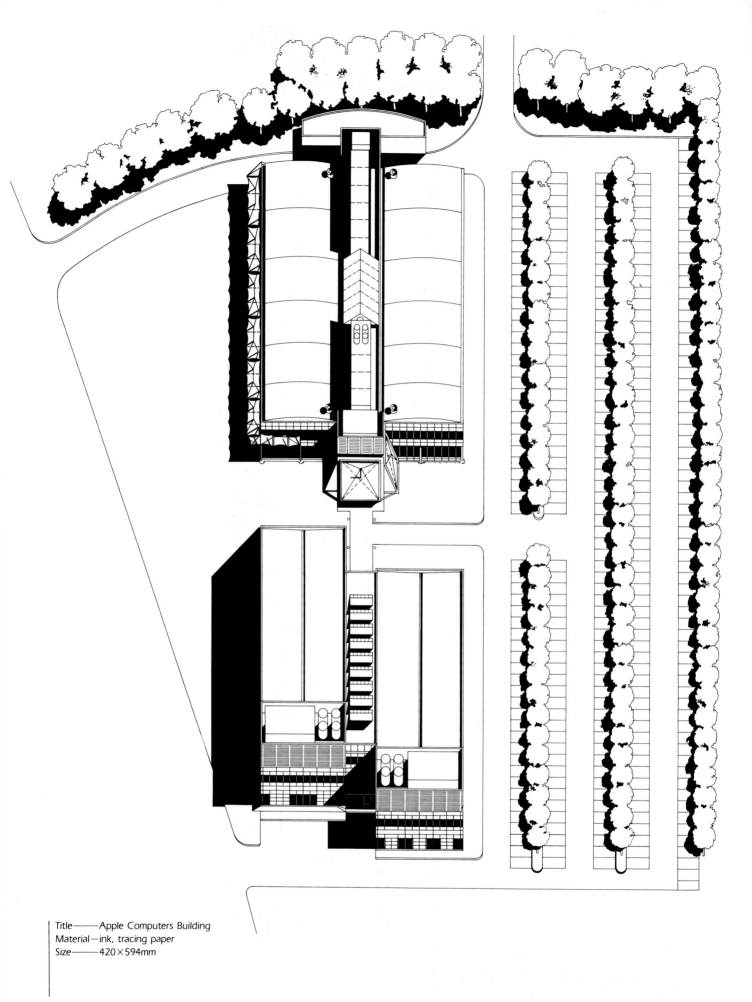

Title———Apple Computers Building
Material—ink, tracing paper
Size———420×594mm

Planometric drawing showing Phase 2 in the
foreground which is on site, and Phase 1 beyond
which is complete.

Title———Acton Vocational Training Centre
Material—ink, tracing paper
Size———594×841mm

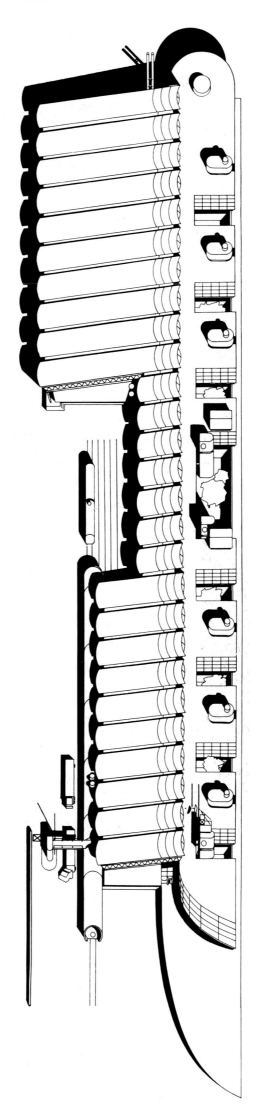

Troughton McAslan was selected for this scheme
following a single stage competition. The project
consists of a 20,000 square metre centralised
training facility for London Underground Ltd (LUL).
Accommodation comprising workshops, classrooms,
a simulated working station, administration and
back-up facilities has been arranged on two floors in
a linear manner either side of a central "internal
street". The building consists of deep steel trusses
and metal cladding for long span areas and a steel
frame with brick and glazed infills for the two-storey
blocks.

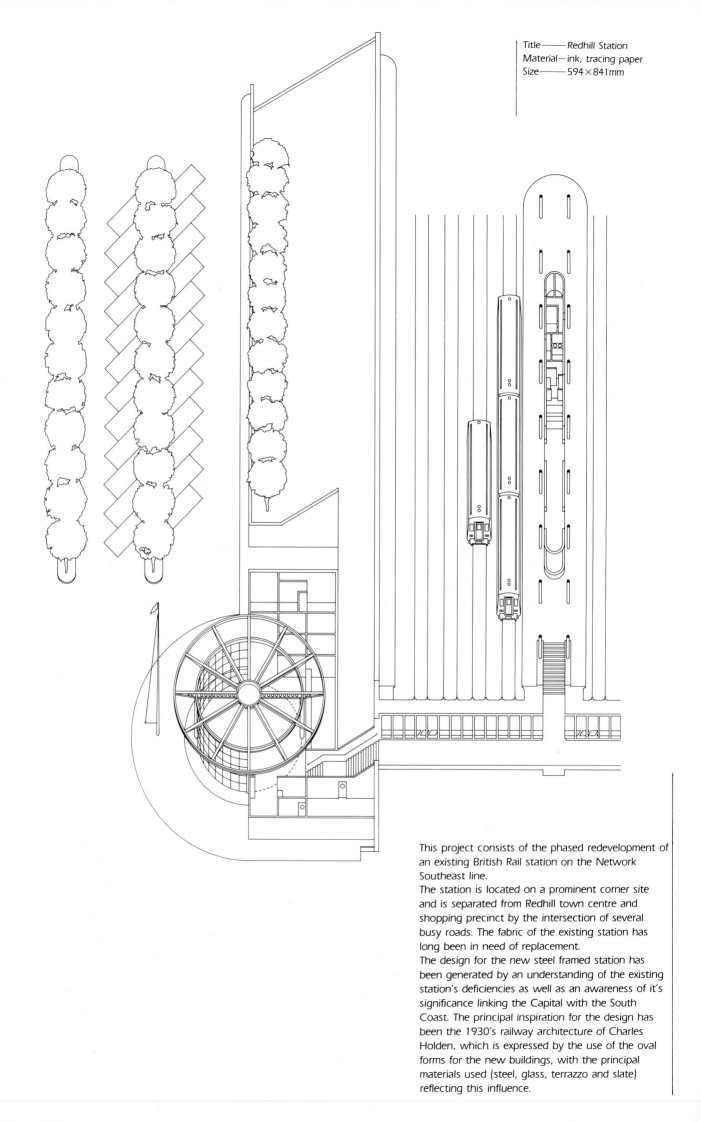

Title——Redhill Station
Material—ink, tracing paper
Size———594×841mm

This project consists of the phased redevelopment of an existing British Rail station on the Network Southeast line.

The station is located on a prominent corner site and is separated from Redhill town centre and shopping precinct by the intersection of several busy roads. The fabric of the existing station has long been in need of replacement.

The design for the new steel framed station has been generated by an understanding of the existing station's deficiencies as well as an awareness of it's significance linking the Capital with the South Coast. The principal inspiration for the design has been the 1930's railway architecture of Charles Holden, which is expressed by the use of the oval forms for the new buildings, with the principal materials used (steel, glass, terrazzo and slate) reflecting this influence.

# Afterword

This essay seeks to further define the imaginary architecture of the 1990s by examining the current form of paper based architecture that was born in England at the beginning of the sixties and is now being developed in the works of youthful professionals.

From the sixties, the Archigram movement developed drawing as an independent form of expression and gave it its own significance within the field of architecture. As typified by the activities of the Beatles, this was an era in which the media became enmeshed in the lives of everyday people as never before. The fact that London, the veritable cradle of pop art, was the scene of Archigram activity may have had an impact. Indeed, by incorporating these influences and taking advantage of the mass media, it completely informationalised the concept of architecture. Although in the past drawings had also been sketched to convey architectural concepts, many of those inspired by this movement never became actual buildings. The fact that Archigram's architects had initially created such drawings to be published and made into images, making the drawings themselves the most important means of their activities, was nothing less than epoch-making.

During this period, such architects did not actually create real work to be constructed, but rather, they used drawing strategically as a criticism of everyday architecture which lacked imagination and of architecture that only expressed the uniform technology of the time. They used it as a means for expressing disappointment in the system that enveloped architecture and in the production system that cast it in an unvarying mould. They used it as a means to offer proposals for a future society and image of the world. This movement had reverberations throughout the world, and in 1966 Super-studio was created, primarily by the students of the Faculty of Architecture at the University of Florence in Italy. It was among a group of classmates at this same University of Florence that Archizoom was born, giving drawing a cartoon type expression, that was both more radical and more comical. This movement exerted a great influence on

Hans Hollein in Australia, and on Isozaki in Japan. In turn, it gave rise to the activities of Raimund Abraham and John Hejduk, leading ultimately to the recent 'architecture as a message' conveyed through the media by such noteworthy talents as Daniel Libeskind, Bernard Tschumi and Zaha Hadid that is still fresh in our minds.

Throughout history, drawing in architecture has been a highly influential tool of communication, often playing a prophetic role. The work of Hugh Ferris in America, who was active during the twenties exemplified this. The American architectural historiographer, Katsuhiro Kobayashi, refers to Ferris as the great spokesman of style during the period that witnessed the creation of the art deco skyscrapers. Ferris first worked as a draughtsman for Cass Gilbert. Then in 1922 he entered into a collaboration with architect Harvey Wiley Corbett to produce a famous four page study, drawing and essay for the 'New York Times'. Later, he published drawings entitled 'An Indication of the Effect of New York's Imaginative Scenery Zoning Law of 1942'. This work was a proposal for a New York street layout following the implementation of the zoning law and it depicted the great force engendered by art deco high-rise architecture. After this, Ferris continued to depict architecture in various forms and the city images that would be created by it. He was a creative stimulus for the architects of his time and fulfilled a role best described as the spark for the skyscrapers of today's New York.

Although Mies Van Der Rohe's drawings known as the 'glass skyscraper proposals' were made for Europe in the twenties, when high rise structures simply could not be built, they did, however, find their perfect expression in the continuous belt-like glass windowed structures that spread through both the United States and Europe following the conclusion of World War II.

The works of Antonio Sant'Elia, which formed the basis for Italy's futuristic faction, were never brought to fruition during his lifetime. Nevertheless, his drawings were eventually a force in bringing Italy into the mainstream of Europe's modern architecture. Moreover, it goes without saying that drawing has had a particularly great mission in Russian structuralism as well. Drawings have been sketched endlessly, providing stimulus to innovators and opening the way to new eras, even in times when the actual structures they foresaw could not be built for political or economic reasons.

The eighties was an era when the originality of authors seemed to expand boundlessly and proliferate by itself. With the flourishing commercialism which resulted from the bubble economy, the paper type architecture of avant-garde architects was transformed into real creations at dizzying speed. However, in contrast to this was a parallel trend towards a loss of strength in terms of originality.

Having passed through this era, drawing in the nineties has now entered a phase of increasing importance. How will it stir our creativity and what sort of proposals will it indicate to us? The nineties may indeed be a period in which we discover in drawing an insight into new values and new concepts.

Hoping to portray drawing on as large a scale as possible, I have put together a collection focusing on about one fifth of the works that have been sent to me by various architects. I cannot thank those architects enough who were so kind as to contribute such excellent work. I have endeavoured to include in my architectural selection as many of these remarkably active young architects as possible. In choosing them I have sought the advice of Mr Deyan Sudjic of 'Blueprint', Mr John Welsh of 'Building Design' and my friend and architect Kathryn Findlay.

As I come to the end of this essay, I would like to express my heartfelt thanks to Andy Smith and Hiroko Naito for their assistance in the organisation and gathering of materials, and also my sincere appreciation to Peter Wilson for contributing a refreshingly splendid text for this work.

**Fumio Shimizu, February 1993**

## Anish Kapoor & David Connor

Anish Kapoor was born in Bombay. His works are deeply hued with a philosophical colouring, said to contrast the earth and the blue sky with empty space. He won the Year 2000 Prize at the Venice Biennale in 1991.

David Connor was born in Birmingham in 1950. Much of the architecture he has dealt with is of a fashionable nature, works influenced by new ornamentalism. In addition, he is experienced with the punk movement.

## Ahrends Burton and Koralek Architects

The partnership has a wide range of experience developed over a period of more than twenty years. During this time, the practice has completed a great variety of projects including planning studies and development plans, housing – both government-financed and private – university and other higher educational buildings, hospitals, schools, libraries, commercial and industrial buildings. Peter Ahrends, Richard Burton and Paul Koralek studied architecture together at the AA in London from 1951 to 1956. Their partnership was effectively established when Paul Koralek won the International Competition for a new library at Trinity College, Dublin in 1961.

## George Antanassiu

George Antanassiu was born in Athens in 1963. He writes that much of his childhood was 'spent between the scatter of materials slowly turning into buildings. There were precious moments when these became fragmented havens of architectural play-places before they were possessed by others'. In 1981 he moved to the UK to study painting and languages. Since 1984 he has studied at the AA and from 1987 with Ada Wilson.

## Apicella Associates

Lorenzo Apicella was born in 1957 in Ravello, Italy and educated at Nottingham University School of Architecture, Canterbury College of Art and the Royal College of Art. In 1982 he gained his RIBA qualification. Between 1981 and 1989 he worked on major skyscaper projects in the USA for Skidmore Owings & Merrill; on lightweight structures and exhibitions in England and Europe for Imagination; on independent interiors and furniture projects and taught at Canterbury School of Architecture. From May 1989 he has been principal of Apicella Associates working on projects ranging from office buildings, lightweight structures, interiors and exhibitions, to a new range of café furniture designed for production in the UK.

## Architekturbüro Bolles-Wilson

Peter Wilson was born in 1950 in Melbourne, Australia. From 1980–1988 he practised as the Wilson Partnersnip with Julia B Bolles-Wilson, and since 1988 he has been a partner in Architekturbüro Bolles-Wilson, London and Münster. Between 1978 and 1988 he was a Unit Master at the AA. His projects include the City Library, Münster (completed 1993), Folly in Osaka (1990) and Blackburn House, London (1987).

## Armstrong Associates

Kenneth Armstrong trained at the Mackintosh School in Glasgow and the Royal College of Art, London, and subsequently worked at Foster Associates where he was involved primarily with the Hong Kong & Shanghai Bank and the winning BBC Competition entry. Before setting up Armstrong Chipperfield in 1984 he worked for DEGW as team coordinator on the feasibility study for the Barclays Bank Headquarters at Radbroke Hall. He has also taught at the Bartlett School of Architecture and lectured at the Royal College of Art.

## Beevor Mull & Associates

Catrina and Robert first met in 1983 in their final year at the AA in Nigel Coates' Unit 10. After graduation they co-founded the NATO group which wrote and published manifestos. They have also run their own architectural practice since 1984. Beginning with small projects predominantly for their circle of friends, they soon expanded their business to larger scale projects for private and commercial concerns. However, Beevor & Mull have no intention of over-expanding the business since their trademark is their personal contact with clients and suppliers. They are currently working on a restaurant, a bar in West London, a warehouse/studio and a private house abroad.

## Avci + Jurca

Avci + Jurca is an integrated design practice established in 1988, headed by E Selcuk Avci and Sanja Jurca Avci with architects, designers and engineers.

The practice believes that the most dynamic response to the complexity of today's buildings is an integrated method where the architect and engineer work as a close team. The client thus receives a unified service where only one line of communication is required. The process of design and construction is therefore more elegant, rapid and efficient, providing the architect with a greater understanding of technology and giving the client a more direct line of involvement with his consultants. With this approach Avci + Jurca aim to break the moulds of standardised solutions to unique design problems. They insist on a particular approach to every brief and a close working relationship with the client in the development of ideas.

The practice has a track record of success in competitions and a collection of awards. It is the policy of Avci + Jurca architects and designers to take part in competitions as a way of facilitating a greater national and international understanding of architectural issues.

## Benedetti Renato Giovanni

Benedetti Renato Giovanni was born in 1962. In 1985 he received the BES and in 1988 the BArch degrees from the University of Waterloo, where he also designed a demountable suspended panel system for the School of Architecture exhibitions. He has worked for various practices in England, Italy and Canada including Munkenbeck & Marshall Architects, London; Emilio Battisti Architects, Milan; and YRM Architects, London.

His own projects include the Pontoon Dock Ideas Competition, London Docklands; a feasibility study for a small mountain hotel in Cyprus; and the expansion and refurbishment of a farmhouse in the mountains near Parma, Italy. He has had drawings exhibited in Rome and at the RIBA in London.

## Ben Kelly Design

Ben Kelly was born in 1949 in Welwyn Garden City and attended the Lancaster School of Art (1966 and 1970) before going on to the Royal College of Art (1971-74) where he obtained an MA and RCA. Building up work experience between 1974 and 1976, he opened Ben Kelly Design in November 1976.

## Carlos Villanueva Brandt

Born in 1957 in Caracas, Venezuela, Carlos Villanueva Brandt moved to England in 1968 and between 1977 and 1982 studied at the AA. In 1983 he became a founder member of NATO. He has been in private Art and Architectural practice since 1984, and since 1983 has been Unit Master teaching design at the AA.

## Benson & Forsyth

Professor Gordon Benson was born in Glasgow in 1944, and Alan Forsyth in Newcastle-Upon-Tyne in the same year. They both graduated from the AA School of Architecture in 1968 and set up a private practice together in 1978. Featuring strongly in various international competitions, they have completed many successful projects from housing estates to the Pavilion for the Glasgow Garden Festival. Current work includes a science market and a commercial development in Glasgow. In addition to running the partnership, they are both involved in academic teaching.

## Raoul Bunschoten

Raoul Bunschoten is an independent architect based in London. He is involved in explorations about the nature of architecture which often result in large installations for various international exhibitions. He is currently involved in writing a series of articles on new definitions of architecture. He teaches at the AA School of Architecture in London, where since 1983 he has been Unit Master of Diploma Unit 2. This unit is in the nature of a laboratory for architecture.

His projects include several urban schemes in the Netherlands, his country of origin. These include

Spinoza's Garden (1985), a project about the building of a new city on new land (Almere in the Flevopolder) and the complete redesign of the Museumplein (1988) – the central square in Amsterdam housing all the museums and the concert halls – including the extension of the Steddeljik Museum and a new theatre for which he won first prize. At this time he was invited to design a project for the Berlin exhibition 'Berlin: Monument or Thought Model?' for which he developed an urban project for the old political centre of Germany, a site bombed during the Second World War and until recently cut in half by the wall.

Most recently, he has worked on a large project called 'The Skin of the Earth', upon the invitation of the Union of Architects of the Soviet Union, which was exhibited in Moscow in 1992.

## Campbell Zogolovitch Wilkinson & Gough Architects

Nick Campbell, Roger Zogolovitch, Rex Wilkinson and Piers Gough all trained together at the AA School in London in the late sixties. They set up their first office in the basement of the school and concentrated on the design of swinging boutiques and private house alterations. The actual partnership (CZWG) was formed in 1975, and much of their early work consisted of conversions. At present, they are involved in a wide range of new-build projects. Their office has expanded to forty-five staff members.

## Nick Coombe

Born in 1958, Nick Coombe studied architecture at Canterbury College of Art and the Royal College of Art, where he graduated in 1983 with the Major Travel Scholarship and the RCA Basil Ward Award.

In Berlin he worked for Alessandro Carlini and in New York assisted the architectural historian Kenneth Frampton. He worked for the designers Powell-Tuck & Connor in London, before setting up his own studio in 1986. Clients have included the fashion entrepreneur Joseph, the fashion company Issey Miyake UK, Abbey Road Recording Studios and the Institute of Contemporary Art. His major commission to date is a large private house in West London for a young media client.

He has lectured and exhibited extensively in Britain. In 1985, he carried out a British Council Research visit to the Soviet Union to study the work of the visionary architect Konstantin Melnikov.

## D'Soto '88 Design Group

Jose Cruzat-Salazar, Ron Brinkers and Ric Zito all studied together as students of Architecture and Design at Kingston Polytechnic and officially set up D'Soto '88 in June 1987. They work in various areas of design including architecture, interiors, exhibition work and graphic design. Their distinctive style stems from several different influences, but it is their own inspiration and enthusiasm for articulated engineering that gives the dynamic expression of technology to their work. Indeed, a common feature of D'Soto's work is visually celebrated junctions and fixings.

## Guy Comely

After studying at the AA, Guy Comely has worked with a series of London architects including Nigel Greenhill and Chris Wilkinson in order to acquire a technical and contractual knowledge of building. Exhibitions in which he has participated include 'Living with Rust' at One-off and '100 Storeys 100 Towers'. He intends to set up his own practice shortly but will continue with private commissions.

## David Chipperfield Architects

Born in 1953 in London, David Chipperfield trained at Kingston Polytechnic and the AA. On graduating he worked for Richard Rogers and Foster Associates. In 1984 he founded David Chipperfield and Partners. The practice has gained a reputation through its interiors and competition designs in England and abroad, and has recently completed two buildings in London – a house for the photographer Nick Knight and some artists' studios. The practice has collaborated wih Skidmore Owings and Merrill, Frank O Gehry and Isozaki and is currently collaborating with Yves Lion on a project in France.

In 1987, the practice opened an office in Tokyo. Executed projects include shops for the fashion designer Issey Miyake, a discothèque, a recently completed private museum in Tokyo and a commercial building in Kyoto. The practice has recently been organised to design a large office building in Okayama.

David Chipperfield is a director and founder member of the 9H Gallery, He has taught at Harvard and is a part-time tutor at the RCA and an external examiner at the Central London Polytechnic.

## Din Associates

Rasshied Ali Din was born in April 1956 and studied at the Birmingham Polytechnic between 1975 and 1979. He worked for three of the UK's top design consultancies before setting up Din Associates in February 1986. Projects completed include an impressive list of shops and department stores, boardrooms and a conference centre.

## David Marks Julia Barfield Architects

David Marks, Julia Barfield and Kieran Breen are the directors of David Marks Julia Barfield Limited. This tightly knit professional team concentrates on a select number of commissions to ensure the original quality of the design. Both the directors and staff share the common goals of demonstrating iniative and enterprise to create successful building projects. This arises from the determination to create quality and good value for money, to understand clearly the client's requirements, to attain a good grasp of the building

process, to demand high performance in materials and details and to recognise the architect's wider responsibility to the user, the passer-by and the environment.

## Catherine 'Du Toit

Catherine 'Du Toit was born in 1963 in Cape Town, South Africa. She received a BA in Architectural Studies from the University of Cape Town where she studied from 1982-84, and the AA diploma from the AA in London which she attended from 1985-88.

## Edward Cullinan Architects

Edward Cullinan Architects started in 1965 as a cooperative partnership working from an open plan converted warehouse in Camden, London and has now grown to a practice of thirty people. The emphasis is very much upon sustaining variety and avoiding the creative freeze of specialisation. The practice tends to work on buildings with unusual briefs or in sensitive environments. A great deal of time is spent on developing and elaborating designs and some of our more sensitive projects have led to large scale public involvement through open meetings. Our completed projects include health care buildings, rennovation of a burnt down nineteenth century church, and recladding of post-war schools.

## Fisher Park Limited

Mark Fisher graduated in architecture from the AA in London. He practiced as a freelance architect and in the early seventies ran the celebrated 'Nice Ideas' unit at the AA. Jonathan Park studied mechanical sciences at Clare College, Cambridge and Imperial College, London. After working with Ove Arup and Arup Associates for a number of years he set up his own engineering practice and ran Diploma Technical Studies at the AA. Their partnership was formed in 1977 and they directed their concentration to special effects in the world of rock and roll. Since then, Fisher Park Limited has expanded to provide a comprehensive design service to the entertainment industry. In addition to show design, they have also covered the design of major international discothèques, leisure attractions, portable theatres and presentations for major public companies.

## William Firebrace

William Firebrace writes of his life and influences: '[I was] conceived in Bar Porcupine, Buenos Aires [and] brought up in Vienna, in a tall house filled with china; lived in a small room lined with wallpaper of green horses. Worked on a farm in England, became dizzy with the noise of the machinery and the sensual smell of grain in the dryers. Read 'A Study in Scarlet' by Sir Arthur Conan Doyle. Climbed to the top of Hawksmoor's church in Spitalfields to the great conical chamber within the spire, occupied by a pigeön, peered out through the grimy windows. Encountered a woman sleeping on a beach wearing swimming goggles, had a conversation. Lay in bed for nine months with a viral illness watching showings of 'The Lone Ranger'. Got up'.

## Pedro Guedes

Pedro Paulo D'Alpoim Guedes was born in 1948 and grew up in Mozambique, East Africa. He studied architecture at Cambridge and since 1978 has been in private practice. He has been Unit Master at the AA for many years. His architectural projects include many competitions, houses, office buildings, public housing, commercial interiors, zoo buildings and exhibitions. Pedro Guedes is currently a member of Pentagram Design in London.

## Zaha Hadid

Zaha Hadid attended the AA and then worked with the Office of Metropolitan Architecture before setting up her own practice. She has worked on several projects at the same time as teaching full-time at the AA, and presently works from a converted Victorian schoolhouse in Clerkenwell, London. She is currently working on an office building and housing block for IBM in Berlin, and a vertical retail building and studio office in Tokyo; the latter of which is soon to commence construction.

## Eva Jiricna Architects

Eva Jiricna qualified as an engineer/architect at the University of Prague in 1962 and received a post-graduate degree from the Prague Academy of Fine Arts in 1963. She came to the UK in 1968 and worked for a year with the GLC Schools Division before becoming an associate with Louis de Soissons Partnership, working on the planning, design and construction programmes for Brighton Marina. She set up her own practice in 1980 with David Hodges and formed Jiricna Kerr Associates in 1985.

## Andrew Holmes

Born in 1947 in Worcestershire, Andrew Holmes was a member of the AA between 1966 and 1972. In 1972 he won first prize for 'The City as a Significant Environment' award and in 1974 that for the RIBA/Rotring Architectural Drawings Award. In addition to this, he has collected the D and AD Silver Award from the Penguin Book of Kites, and between 1980 and 1982 worked on the invention and design of the new Bus Map for London Transport. He has worked as an architect, interior designer and graphic architect since 1974, and became Unit Master at the AA, London, in 1985. He is represented in several public and private collections, including the RIBA Drawings Collection.

## Herron Associates

In a spectacular career that has stretched from 1954 when he became an architect with the Greater London Council, Ron Herron has become a major international design figure. During the early sixties he was one of the small group of architects that designed London's Hayward Gallery and the Queen Elizabeth Hall. Having worked with many of the UK's top design consultancies, he established Herron Associates in 1982. He has also held the position of tutor at the AA in London since 1965.

## Feilden Clegg Design

High quality buildings are the primary objective of Feilden Clegg where the stress is very much on good design and management skills. Client liaison is close and the aim is to provide leadership and solutions to problems. The practice has worked with a wide range of clients from community groups to educational establishments, local authorities and commercial developers.

## Leon Krier

Born in 1946 in Luxembourg, Leon Krier studied at the University of Stuttgart from 1967-68. Between 1968 and 1974 he was assistant to James Stirling in London. He taught Architecture and Urbanism at the AA and the Royal College of Art in London, and also at Princeton University from 1974-77. In 1982, he was Jefferson Professor at UVA. In 1977 he was awarded the Berlin Prize for Architecture (with Rob Krier), in 1985 he received the Jefferson Memorial Medal and in 1987 the Chicago Annual AIA Award.

Leon Krier has lived and worked in London since 1968. In November 1988 he was appointed by HRH The Prince of Wales as masterplanner of the Poundbury Development in Dorset which covers 450 acres. In conjunction with Rob Krier, he is currently planning a twenty-hectare urban quarter in San Sebastian, Spain.

## Flashman Associates

Geraldine Flashman was born in 1960 and graduated from the Royal College of Art's School of Architecture and Design. She founded Flashman Associates in 1987. The practice is intent upon producing high quality modern architecture and design that reflects contemporary techniques and construction methods. Flashman Associates has undertaken projects which range from residential and commercial to cultural, and has built for itself a reputation of producing high quality work with a disciplined adherence to excellent detailing. Geraldine Flashman has taught Architecture at the University of London and currently holds a lectureship in Architecture and Design at the Royal College of Art.

## Ian Ritchie Associates

Ian Ritchie was born in England and trained at the School of Architecture in Liverpool between 1965 and

1972. He worked for Foster Associates for four years before setting up independently in the UK and in France. He was one of the founder members of Chrysalis Architects, and set up Ian Ritchie Associates in London. The firm concentrates on lightweight structures, passive solar energy, art and technology. His work has received many awards and has been widely published and exhibited. He has also lectured and taught in the UK, France and Japan.

## Spencer Fung

Spencer Fung received both a BA and an MA from Churchill College, Cambridge and won the first prize in the fifth RIBA International Student Competition in 1987. Between 1980 and 1986 he gained professional experience working on projects throughout the world for practices including Wong Ouyang Associates (Hong Kong) and David Chipperfield and Partners (London). His work includes the National Rowing Museum (Henley-on-Thames), the Admiralty Commercial Centre (Hong Kong) and many projects in England, the United States, France, Saudi Arabia, Singapore and Indonesia. He has also published projects in various journals and teaches design at the North London Polytechnic.

## Florian Beigal Architects

Florian Beigal was born in 1941 in Konstanz, West Germany. He studied architecture at the University of Stuttgart from 1962- 68 and at the Bartlett School of Architecture and Planning, London University, from 1968-69. His professional work, undertaken by the Architecture Bureau which he formed with Peter Rich and Jon Broome, ranges from involvement in the Munich Olympic structures of 1968 to working on the Half Moon Theatre in London.

## Ada Gansach-Wilson

Ada Gansach-Wilson studied at the AA and was awarded the Eileen Gray Scholarship in 1980 and the AA Diploma (Hons) in 1981. She has worked in Brussels, Amsterdam, Paris, Istanbul, Ahmedabad, Vijayanagar, Kathmandu and London and is currently a partner in Design Emphasis, a private practice established in 1983. She has also been Unit Master at the AA since 1988.

## Amarjit Kalsi

Born in 1957 in Nairobi, Kenya, Amarjit Kalsi was educated at the AA in London between 1975 and 1981. During this period he began to work for the Richard Rogers Partnership and was appointed one of the directors a few years ago. His interests in the practice are varied. He likes the process of design – from concepts through to details – and enjoys the exploration of ideas through drawings. He also plays an active role in the management of the practice, believing both activities complement one another.

## Justina Karakiewicz

Justina Karakiewicz was born in Cracow, Poland and came to London in 1975. Between 1975 and 1978 she studied at the Central London Polytechnic and from 1978-80 at the AA School of Architecture. She has worked for various architectural practices including EPR Partnership, the Austin Company of UK Ltd and Rock Townsend before starting on her own in 1985. She has taught at the AA since 1984 as external tutor and full-time tutor at Intermediate School Unit 13. She has also been visiting critic at Bath University, North London Polytechnic and Ecole D'Architecture Paris-Villemin.

## Munkenbeck + Marshall Architects

Alfred Munkenbeck [BA (Hons), MAR(Harv), RIBA] studied at Le Rosey, Dartmouth and Harvard USA. He has worked with James Stirling and Partners, Foster Associates, Jose Luis Sert and Harrison Abramovitz. He is design critic at the Boston Architectural Centre, the AA and Cambridge University.

Stephen Marshall [B Arch (Hons), MAR (Harv), RIBA] studied at Strathclyde and was awarded the Harkness Fellowship to Harvard. He has worked with Farrell Grimshaw Partnership, IM Pie Inc and as a partner in Aylward Laing Marshall Robson. He is visiting critic at South Bank Polytechnic, Strathclyde and Plymouth.

The partnership of Munkenbeck + Marshall developed from an amalgamation of experience in prestige European and large Middle Eastern projects. The practice also has particular expertise in the programming and design of schools, industrial cost-in-use studies and the planning of large scale urban developments.

## Neave Brown David Porter Architects

Neave Brown was born in New York in 1929 and studied at the AA. His major projects include housing at Winscombe Street, Alexandra Road and Fleet Road, all in Camden, London. He is a visiting Professor at the Cornell, Princeton, St Louis and Carnegie Mellon Universities in the USA.

David Porter was born in 1946, and studied architecture at the Bartlett School, joining Neave Brown to work on the Fleet Road Project.

## Nicholas Grimshaw & Partners Ltd

Nicholas Grimshaw graduated with honours from the AA School of Architecture in 1965 and has been in private practice since then. His present firm, Nicholas Grimshaw & Partners Ltd, was established in 1980. Nicholas Grimshaw built up his reputation in the field of industrial architecture during the 1970s when he received the Financial Times Award for Industrial Architecture and a RIBA award for his work on the Herman Miller building in Bath. Since the establishment of his present firm he has widened his scope to include sports and leisure complexes, commercial and retail buildings, and projects in the field of television and radio.

### Rick Mather Architects

Rick Mather Architects maintains a varied architectural and planning practice focusing upon institutional, residential and commercial work. Notable projects include: the Schools of Education and Information Systems and the Climatic Research Unit at the University of East Anglia, Norwich; the Zen Restaurants in London, Hong Kong and Montreal; and the major renovation of the AA in Bedford Square, London. Work in progress or recently completed includes: a 500 unit residential development for the University of East Anglia; the new master plan for the expansion of the University of East Anglia; a 105,000 square-foot office development near London Bridge; Point West, a 400 apartment development in South Kensington, London; the Latif residential compound in Khartoum; the expansion of the Zen restaurants to Hong Kong and North America; the Waddington Sculpture Gallery, Cork Street, London; the design of the new South Quay Station complex for the Docklands Light Rail; and the winning scheme in the London Docklands Development Corporation competition for the new restaurant complex at Millwall Dock.

Rick Mather is also a RIBA external examiner at the University of Cambridge and the Polytechnic of Central London. He has taught at the Bartlett School, London University, the AA and recently at the Harvard Graduate School of Design in Cambridge, Massachusetts.

The work of Rick Mather Architects has been published and exhibited widely, including exhibitions at Art Net, the 9H Gallery, the Harvard Graduate School of Design, and L'Institut Francais D'Architecture in Paris. The firm received Architectural Design Awards in 1982 and 1984 and a RIBA award in 1988.

### Stanton Williams

Alan Stanton graduated with an honours diploma from the AA in London and received an MA in Architecture and Urban Design from the University of California, Los Angeles. He is also a member of the RIBA and a Medallist of the Societé des Architectes Diplome par le Government, Paris.

Paul Williams has a BA (Hons) and an MA in 3D Design from Birmingham College of Art and is a Research Fellow in Museum and Gallery Design at the Yale Arts Centre, USA.

Current projects being undertaken by Stanton Williams include the design of a new wing for the National Portait Gallery, the design of a new museum in Winchester Cathedral and a master plan for the development of Hawksmoor's Church and site in St George-in-the-East, London.

### Stirling Wilford and Associates

Born in 1926, James Stirling studied at the Liverpool School of Art and the School of Architecture at Liverpool University. He started in private practice in 1956 and officially set up with Michael Wilford in 1971. Sadly, in June 1992 James Stirling passed away.

Michael Wilford was born in Surbiton, Surrey in 1938 and studied at Kingston Technical School, the Northern Polytechnic School of Architecture, London and the Regent Street Polytechnic Planning School, London. Although he worked with James Stirling from 1960 it was not until 1971 that they set up business together.

### Melanie Sainsbury Associates

Melanie Sainsbury was born in London in 1956 and trained at the Polytechnic of Central London and the AA. On graduating she worked with her former professor Nigel Coates, assisting him with several commissions including Jasper Conran's house in London. She was a founder member of the NATO group in 1983.

In 1985 Melanie set up her own architectural practice working on residential and retail projects in London for Shirley and Tom Conran, an artist's studio for the painter Christopher Brooks and a flat for Beth Rothschild. The practice has also been commissioned frequently to design and manufacture specialist lights and architectural accessories such as a lighting design for Fred's Night-club in Soho, London, commissioned by Tchaik Chassay.

More recently, Melanie's projects have included a commission to put forward ideas for the Spaghetti Juntion intersection in Birmingham for the BBC's 'Late Show' in June 1990.

### Johnathon Sergison

Johnathon Sergison was born in 1964 and studied at Canterbury School of Architecture, graduating in 1986. Here he was awarded the Antony Wade prize for best degree student. He then studied at the AA under Rodrigo Perez d'Arce and graduated in 1989. He has worked for various practices in London including Armstrong Associates, Antony Hunt Engineers and Tony Fretton Architects. He assisted at the 9H Gallery (1987-89) and in 1989 assisted Alvaro Siza on the Paris National Library competition.

His independent work includes entries for the Joshua Reynolds Competition in 1986 (with Lorenzo Apicella), the Waterloo International Competition in 1989 and the Acropolis Museum Competition in 1990 (with Marios Economides and Dafna Arnon).

### Doug Patterson

Doug Patterson studied at Hornsey College of Art & Design and was awarded a first class honours degree. From here he studied at the Royal College of Art, graduating in 1972 with an MA, and then at the AA, gaining a diploma in architecture. During the past fourteen years he has worked on a wide variety of projects ranging from architecture to film set design. He is a partner in Patterson Hewitt & Partners Ltd, Design Consultants.

Doug Patterson's drawings have been widely published, and during the past four years he has been working on a series of architectural illustrations. The inspiration for the series came whilst travelling in Portugal, Spain, India, Egypt, Italy and England; from the buildings of the Maharajas, the architecture of the British Raj, the temples of Luxor, the palladian villas of the Veneto and the numerous follies and bizarre buildings in England, from Blackpool Tower to some of the finest country houses.

### Kay Ngee Tan with Christopher McCarthy

Kay Ngee Tan was born in 1956 in Singapore. He first started to write at the age of fifteen – mainly prose, short stories and film reviews. In 1977 his collected essays Never Ending Summer were published and in the same year he first encountered architecture. In 1984 he graduated from the AA in London. He was a prize winner in the RIBA International Students competition in 1985 and won the AJ/Bovis Awards in 1987. Between 1984 and 1990 he worked for Arup Associates. In the meantime, writings, films and architecture still intermingle to create new findings.

Christopher D'Esterre McCarthy is a senior structural engineer in Ove Arup and Partners. He has worked on large span structures including sports halls, exhibition halls, warehouses, railway terminals, bridges and recently a transfer structure supporting high-rise buildings over a road. He is a sculptor in spirit who believes firmly in pursuing the holistic balance between visual function and physical function in structural forms.

### Peter Mance

Born in 1963 in Evesham, Peter Mance left school at sixteen to become a builder's apprentice for two years from 1980-82. He returned to education and undertook a two year B/TEC Diploma course at Hereford College of Art and Design, before attending Kingston Polytechnic between 1984 and 1987, where he graduated with BA (Hons) in Interior Design. Since graduation, Peter Mance has been a self-employed designer, working predominantly alongside Ben Kelly.

### Louisa Hutton/Matthias Sauerbruch Architects

Born in 1957, Louisa Hutton gained a first class degree from Bristol University in 1980. She then worked with Edward Samuel & Partners in London during 1981, before studying at the AA where she was awarded the diploma in 1984. From 1984-87 she worked with A & P Smithson and gained her RIBA qualification. She has taught at Croydon College of Art from 1987-88 and at the AA since 1988. Since 1987 she has worked with Matthias Sauerbruch.

Matthias Sauerbruch was born in 1955 in Germany.

He studied first at the Hochschule der Kunster in Berlin, gaining a diploma in 1984, and then at the AA. He has worked with the Office for Metropolitan Architecture (OMA), London, since 1984 and since 1985 has taught as a Unit Master at the AA.

### Rik Nijs

Rik Nijs was born in 1962 in Belgium. He graduated in 1986 from the Saint Lucas Institute, Belgium, as a technical designer and architect. He then studied Architectural Sciences in History and Theory at the Katholieke Universiteit in Leuven, Belgium, and at the AA in London he studied with Rodrigo Perez de Arce and Micha Bandini.

His recent work includes first prize in the International Ideas Competition (1989) – to improve the site of the Battle of Waterloo, and an entry for the New Acropolis Museum Competition, Athens (1990). This work has been widely published and exhibited at the International Designers Weekend in Brussels and in an exhibition of young architects' work in 1990 at the Architectural Museum in Ghent.

### Tim Ronalds

Tim Ronalds was born in 1950 in London. He studied architecture at Cambridge University and at Massachusetts Institute of Technology between 1968 and 1974. He has taught at the AA since 1977 and at Harvard University from 1990-1991. In 1982 he established his own practice, Tim Ronalds Associates. Their work has been published in 'Japan Architect', 'Architects Journal', 'Country Life' and 'A3 Times'. Projects have been exhibited at RIBA in 1977; at the Royal Academy in 1986, 1988 and 1989; at the Salon International de l'Architects (Paris) in 1990 and in Reality and Project: Four British Architects (London) in 1990.

### Pawson & Silvestrin

John Pawson was born in Halifax, Yorkshire in 1948. After joining the family business between 1968 and 1974, he continued his studies at the Nagoya University of Commerce in Japan and the AA in London. He joined forces with Claudio Silvestrin in 1982.

Claudio Silvestrin was born in 1954 and trained in Milan under Professor AG Fronzoni, the master of Italian 'Architectura Essenziale'. He later moved to the University of Philosophy at Bologna and the AA in London. Before going into partnership with John Pawson in 1982, he was involved with several independent projects and a number of projects with John Hardy. The practice split in April 1989.

### Pierre D'Avoine Architects

Pierre D'Avoine Architects aim at a rigorous approach to work based upon a desire to build. A broad based holistic approach is taken which seeks to go beyond the philosophy, culture and history of the West for inspiration and affirmation. The practice tries to create appropriate environments, which involves a close creative relationship between the client and everyone working on the design and construction process. In an increasingly fragmented world it is necessary to make an architecture that offers a sense of order amidst the chaos.

### Terry Farrell & Company Ltd
The practice was founded in 1965 as the Farrell Grimshaw Partnership. From 1980 it continued in the name of Terry Farrell and Company. During this time the company has developed an international reputation for a diverse range of projects which include interiors, new buildings, refurbishment, restoration and major urban design and town planning projects.

The company has a particular strength in urban design and is recognised for its sensitive and contextural solutions to urban design problems. At present, the practice is involved in many major urban projects in London, Edinburgh and France where it has particular expertise and experience. Their method of working is always tailored to the specific client and project, and takes an active pleasure in the working collaboration between client and other bodies to bring projects to a successful conclusion.

### George Katodrytis
George Katodrytis was born in Cyprus in 1959, and has lived in Britain since 1980. He studied architecture at Manchester University and graduated from the AA in 1985. He worked for Bernard Tschumi in Paris, on the Parc de la Villette, and for various London practices. His work has been exhibited in the UK and Australia and published in design magazines. He has lectured and been visiting critic in various London schools and institutions and has taught at the AA since 1986. Since 1988 George Katodytis has had his own practice GK Architecture/Design, and is currently building two houses and an urban park.

### Mark Pimlott
Mark Pimlott was born in 1958 in Montreal, Canada. He was educated at the McGill University (Montreal) and achieved an Architecture BSc with distinction. He graduated with honours from the AA, London, gaining the Diploma in 1985. His projects have been exhibited at the AA, Arup Associates and RIBA. He taught as a Unit Master at the AA from 1989-90.

### Tony Fretton Architects
Tony Fretton was educated at the AA School of Architecture from 1966-72 and graduated with the AA diploma. In 1974 he qualified as a RIBA Chartered Architect. He has worked for Arup Associates, Neylan and Ungless Architects and Chapman Taylor Partners Architects before setting up his own practice. From 1978-79 he taught at the Bartlett School of Architecture, and from 1980-82 and 1988-89 for two spells at

the AA. He is a guest critic at Princeton, Sci-Arch, Los Angeles and Parsons School of Art, New York.

### Peter Sabara
Peter JB Sabara (BES, AA Diploma) was born in Canada in 1960. He has worked extensively with Branson Coates Architecture on projects in Britain and Japan, and currently teaches at the AA in London as joint Unit Master of Intermediate Unit 9 with Peter Thomas.

### Wickham & Associates Architects
The Wickham & Associates practice was established in 1971 by Julyan Wickham. Since the firm was created they have accepted commissions that range from the interior design of bars, restaurants and clubs as well as many residential interiors, a clinic and planning studies for the Covent Garden Market and Banstead Hospital. They are currently involved in a wide range of work that includes planning studies, interior fitting, a new city block by Tower Bridge, a block of flats, two office buildings and two factories.

### Kevin Rhowbotham
Kevin Rhowbotham was born in 1953. In 1978 he graduated from Oxford Polytechnic achieving a distinction in his Architectural Diploma in 1978. While studying, he was included in the School Prize in Design from 1972-75. He has received many awards and been widely published and exhibited.

### Powell-Tuck Connor + Orefelt Ltd
This practice was established in 1976, concentrating mainly on architecture, landscaping and interior and furniture design. It has been involved in work ranging from a specially commissioned new-build luxury house and studios in California, shop design in Taiwan, new-build offices and studios in London to recording studios, private housing and the design of chairs and light fittings.

### Simon Conder Associates
Simon Conder was trained at the AA and the Royal College of Art in the Industrial Design Department. He worked in the public sector of Basildon New Town between 1975 and 1982, and then moved on to the London Borough of Lambeth. He established his own practice in 1982.

The earlier years of this new practice were dominated by conversion projects, including conversion work on listed houses, but since 1984 the scale of the workload has expanded to include new-build projects and interior design work ranging between 600 and 150,000 square feet.

### Trevor Horne Architects
Trevor Horne is an Englishman who has lived abroad. He studied architecture at the University of Toronto

and has been responsible for work in large practices in Britain and Canada. He entered private practice in 1983 after taking first prize in the University of Durham Oriental Museum Competition. He is a tutor and a visiting critic in various colleges and universities throughout the world, and has had several of his works published in both English and foreign journals.

### Martin Smith

Martin Smith (BSc, B Arch, RIBA) studied at Bath University from 1978-84. Since graduation he has worked in the commercial and industrial sectors of architectural practice. He is committed to assessing each particular project in terms of its location and relevant typology. This has often meant drawing on the historical reservoir of English architecture, but without resorting to pastiche.

Recent built projects include a business centre refurbishment of a large house, a twenty bedroomed hotel within a rural conservation area, a wine bar and the fitting out of a restaurant. Martin Smith is currently working with the Peter Manning Design Group in Leamington Spa.

### Peter Thomas

Peter Thomas was born in 1959 in Taunton, Devon. He was educated at the AA from 1979-86 where he was awarded the AA Diploma (Hons). Since 1988 he has been a Unit Master of the Intermediate Unit 9 at the AA with Peter Sabara.

### Stefano 'De Martino

Stefano 'De Martino has an office in London and teaches in the Diploma School at the AA. A graduate of UCL and the AA (1979) he has worked with OMA (1979-83) and in partnership with Alex Wall (1984-89) collaborating in both teaching and project work. He is currently working on a proposal for offices (with Rem Koolhaas) and various residential projects in London. Collected from his sketch books, the drawings submitted here have not been published before, and reflect in a condensed form some of the ideas developed in his project work in the last few years.

### Tom Heneghan With Inga Dagfinnsdottir

Tom Heneghan graduated from the AA with a diploma in 1975. He has won many awards including first prize in the Art into Landscape Competition (UK) Award in 1980 and a distinction in the Waterloo International Competition (Belgium) in 1989. His projects have been exhibited at the AA, Art Net and the Institute for Contemporary Architecture in London. He teaches at the AA as a Unit Master, at the University of Bath and at University College, London.

Inga Dagfinnsdottir graduated from the AA with a Diploma in 1985, and was included in the Bridge of the Future International Competition (UK) in 1988. Inga's projects have been widely exhibited at the AA and at the Venice Biennale.

### Weil and Taylor

Daniel Weil was born in Buenos Aires, Argentina, in 1953. He graduated in architecture from the University of Buenos Aires in 1977 and then moved to London to continue his studies at the Royal College of Art. He graduated in 1981 and started his own electronics manufacturing company, Parenthesis Limited. Between 1983 and 1985 he was Unit Master at the AA with Nigel Coates.

Gerard Taylor was born in Glasgow in 1955. He studied design at the Glasgow School of Art before graduating in industrial design from the Royal College of Art. After working for the BBC, he moved to Milan where he worked with Sottsass Associati from 1982 until 1985.

Weil and Taylor was established in 1985 and since then they have worked in areas of interior architecture, retail design, industrial design and furniture design for clients in the UK, Europe, America and Japan.

### Will Alsop & John Lyall Architects

Will Alsop was born in Northampton in 1947, and John Lyall in Essex in 1949. They established the practice together in January 1981 and have built up a reputation for interesting architecture at low costs. They are well known in Germany and France as a result of this reputation, and the practice is steadily expanding. The number of architects working for the practice fluctuates from time to time, but is usually about ten people.

The practice split up in August 1991.

### Williams & Hawley Architects

Angela Williams was born in Yorkshire in 1949. In 1973 she graduated from the AA School of Architecture and went on to spend six years working with both Neylan and Ungless, and Levitt Bernstein and Partners designing and building residential projects in Central London and London Docklands before setting up practice in 1979.

Peter Hawley was born in Manchester in 1944. In 1969 he graduated from the University of Strathclyde, Glasgow and went on to spend two years working in both Glasgow and Edinburgh before moving to London. He worked with the London Borough of Lambeth on inner city housing schemes; with Martin Richardson on projects in Milton Keynes; and with Rick Mather Associates and Gerd Kaufmann on the inner city renewal of large derelict Victorian industrial buildings before joining his wife Angela.

Williams & Hawley Architects was established as a practice in 1979. From its inception until the summer of 1988, the practice operated from a studio in Highgate where both partners dealt with a wide variety of commissions. These included individual clients, studios and workshops, community projects, a dental group practice, work on historic buildings and commercial/residential projects with a major national developer based in London.

The policy of the practice has always been to stay small in order to enable the partners to give individual attention to all stages of each commission, in a studio atmosphere and occasionally in collaboration with colleagues. In 1988 the practice moved to Edinburgh. Peter Hawley has taught in the Architectural departments of both the Strathclyde and Heriot Watt Universities. Williams & Hawley have converted their own flat and studio in Edinburgh, which was awarded the Edinburgh Architectural Association Award for 1990. The practice is now looking to expand its work opportunities in Scotland.

## Philip Michael Wolfson

Philip Michael Wolfson was born in 1958 in Philadelphia, USA. He was educated at the Cornell University School of Architecture, Ithaca, USA from 1976-1978, and at the AA in London between 1978 and 1982.

## Troughton McAslan

Jamie Troughton graduated from Cambridge University in 1975 and subsequently worked for Foster Associates and Richard Rogers & Partners.

John McAslan received his training at Edinburgh University and worked in Boston, USA, for two years from 1978. He returned to the UK in 1980 and worked for Richard Rogers & Partners before establishing Troughton McAslan Limited with Jamie Troughton in 1983. The workload is split evenly between the two, with Jamie Troughton concentrating on coordinates, financial and planning matters, and John McAslan specialising in design and project management.